British Railway Signalling

G. M. Kichenside Associate IRSE
Alan Williams

London
IAN ALLAN LTD

Contents

First published 1963
Fourth edition 1978

ISBN 0 7110 0898 1

Published by Ian Allan Ltd, Shepperton, Surrey
and printed in the United Kingdom by
The Press at Coombelands, Addlestone, Surrey

Introduction

Railway signalling is a fascinating subject—fascinating because anyone journeying by train or watching trains from a vantage point near signals can observe the working of the signalling system. Regular travellers on mechanically-signalled lines, without any special interest in railways, soon learn that when the signal arm at the end of the platform is horizontal they may have some time to wait before the train arrives, but if the arm is inclined at 45 degrees up or down the train can be expected within a few minutes. Commuters in large cities know that signals for their train do not have arms but only coloured lights—red, yellow and green—rather like traffic lights on the road but upside down, for the red light is nearly always at the bottom.

Yet there is an air of mystery about railway signalling, for the signals themselves are only part of the story. Much of the interest in signalling lies in the behind-the-scenes procedure carried out in the signalbox before the signals can be cleared for a train. If a mechanical signalbox is on or near the platform, the keen railway enthusiast can learn more about train movements by identifying the signalling bell codes. These are the bell signals sent from signalbox to signalbox to keep the signalmen advised of the passage of trains through the areas they control. The bells give code rings, which are quickly interpreted by the signalman in the same way as a radio operator understands the morse code, but which are meaningless to most people unconnected with railways.

In the last 10 years big strides have been made in the extension of modern power signalling with centralised control. In some areas passengers can stand on stations today and watch points change and signals clear from red to yellow or green but the signalling can be operated from a control panel 50 or more miles away. How this is done is described in the chapter on power signalling.

In this publication we have endeavoured to explain the procedure followed for the safe working of trains on British Railways in terms which can be understood by both the newest recruit to the already large, but growing, band of those having an interest in railways, and the more senior enthusiast who, perhaps, has paid but little attention to railway signalling in the past. Throughout, we have concentrated on the operational side of signalling—how, why and when a signalman carries out the routine, but not how the equipment itself functions, for that comes within the realms of signal engineering, an allied, but for the purposes of this book, too technical a subject. In some cases where technicalities have been unavoidable to assist in the explanation, the description has been given as simply as possible. In the examples of working between signalboxes the names given to signalboxes are fictitious and should not be regarded as necessarily applying to any real box of the same name.

The authors are indebted to British Railways for the provision of facilities in visiting signalboxes from time to time and from which much of the detail in this publication is based and for permitting publication of the emergency working details. Nevertheless, it should be made clear that the book is in no way an official publication of the BRB. The authors also acknowledge the assistance of R. A. Stokes.

G. M. KICHENSIDE, ALAN WILLIAMS

A Southern Region 4-VEP unit restarts from Surbiton past a standard four-aspect junction signal for diverging routes to both the left and right. The train is signalled across to the adjacent right-hand running line, and the five appropriate 'lunar' lights above the signal are therefore illuminated. Note the signal number (S10) and the drivers' telephone at the base of the signal post.

[Alan Williams

1—Development of British Signalling

From the earliest days of railways it was realised that some form of signalling would be required to control the movement of trains. Until the coming of the railway and the introduction of steam power, horses were the most common means of transport over land, in teams harnessed to wagons or coaches, travelling at from 3 to 15 mph, or singly with a mounted rider, and galloping at speeds of 20 to 30 mph. Yet even at these speeds a horse could stop quickly and, on the road, a horse-drawn coach could be steered to avoid a collision with another coach or an obstruction. A train on a fixed line of rails was a very different matter, for its higher speed, heavier load and sole reliance on hand brakes on the engine and on one or two vehicles in the train made it difficult to stop quickly. Thus some means of signalling was necessary to indicate to an engine driver whether he had to stop his train or could continue at speed. Each railway company employed policemen posted at stations, junctions, road level crossings and intermediately where necessary to control the running of trains. They signalled to drivers by hand signals—one arm held sideways for clear, one arm raised above the head for caution and both arms raised above the head for stop.

Almost from the start many railway companies organised their policemen on a similar basis to the then new Metropolitan Police. Their duties included the general maintenance of law and order on railway premises, the inspection of the way and works, the removal of trespassers from the line and assistance in the working of the station, in addition to the operation of points and the signalling of trains. There was no means of communication between policemen at adjacent stations, and trains were run on a time-interval basis. After the passage of a train, the policeman would show a danger signal for a stipulated period to stop another train following the first too closely. When the prescribed time had elapsed (perhaps five minutes), the policeman displayed a caution signal if a second train approached, to indicate to the driver that he must slow down. Finally, after a further period of time (probably another five minutes) he could show a clear signal to allow a following train to proceed. Watches or clocks were then not the common items that they are today and policemen were often issued with sand timers. Thus, in theory, a ten-minute (or other period of time according to location) interval was maintained between trains. Few lines in fact had such a frequent service except at the approaches to principal stations where two or three routes converged and ran over one set of tracks to the station. The policemen had no means of knowing if a train had stopped out of course from a breakdown or other cause, and could easily display a clear signal to a second train when, in fact, the train in front had stopped, perhaps only a mile or so ahead. In such cases the guard of the failed train was supposed to run back to stop a following train. When a train was overdue an engine was sometimes sent out to look for it, but running in the wrong direction on the line on which the missing train should have been approaching. Often the train was found—all too suddenly, and running at speed—and the searching engine had to be reversed quickly to avoid a head-on collision. Although such methods of working were primitive in the extreme, accidents were not as frequent as might be expected, although some were serious and caused casualties.

By the beginning of the 1840s the railway traffic policemen's duties were concentrated more on the working of signals and points for the control of trains and less on other matters which were taken over by other staff. At some of the larger stations they were assisted by pointsmen who set by hand the points needed to switch a train through a complicated route. By this time, too, various forms of fixed signals had been developed to replace hand signals, on the running lines at least, although hand signals, amended in meaning, survive to this day for use in shunting and in an emergency. Fixed signals were of various types—flags mounted in frames, flat boards or discs, or even a solid ball, raised or lowered or mounted on a swivelling device to give the appropriate indications. Two indications were often used—stop and proceed—but these types of signal usually suffered by the fact that only one indication was displayed positively, the other meaning being denoted by the absence of the signal. For example, a rectangular board mounted on a post and displaying its full face towards the driver meant stop but the board was turned through 90 degrees to indicate clear. Thus its edge was turned towards an approaching train and was invisible at a distance. In other cases, the absence of a signal indicated danger. Practice varied from railway to railway and sometimes from section to section. The Great Western introduced one of the earliest fixed signals, the disc and crossbar, which showed a definite indication for both stop and clear. The crossbar for stop was mounted at right angles to the disc for clear and the unit was turned through 90 degrees so that one face or the other was always shown to an approaching train. The signal was mounted at the top of a tall mast to give the driver of a train a clear view of it from a distance and permit him to adjust the train's speed if necessary before reaching the signal.

In 1841 the semaphore signal was adopted by the London & Croydon Railway and, soon after, was used by several other companies. The semaphore arm was pivoted within a slotted post and the indications given by the different positions of the arm: horizontal—stop; diagonally downwards at 45 degrees—caution; vertical (in fact invisible inside the slot in the post)—clear. Sometimes the arms applying to tracks of opposing directions were mounted on the same post but drivers could identify their own signal, for the one which applied to them protruded from the left of the post. At night, coloured lights, worked in conjunction with the semaphore arms, provided the indications: red—stop, green—caution, white—clear. Points and signals were still generally operated by individual levers or handles at the site although in a few instances where lines were complicated or traffic frequent, signals were worked by ropes from a short distance away to allow one man to work say two signals from one position.

The grouping of signal and point levers together in one frame was first seen in the mid-1850s and, although one or two experiments with elementary forms of interlocking between signal and point levers had appeared, the first installation in which levers were interlocked so that signals could be cleared only when the points were correctly set was brought into service in 1860 at Kentish Town. Thus evolved the signalbox, soon located at almost every station and junction.

But the majority of railways still operated trains on the time-interval system. Although the development of the electric telegraph by which messages could be sent electrically over a distance coincided with the early years of railway expansion, few companies made use of it, either because they could not afford the

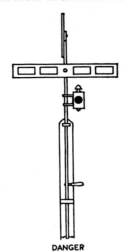

FIG 1 A disc and cross-bar signal used by the GWR from about 1840.

DANGER

CLEAR

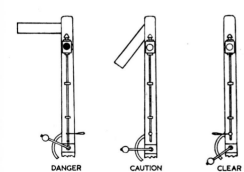

DANGER   CAUTION   CLEAR

FIG 2 A slotted-post three-position semaphore signal, first used by the London & Croydon Railway in 1841.

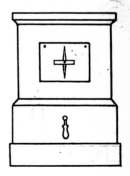

FIG 3 A needle telegraph instrument which was adapted for use in the railway block telegraph system.

cost of installation or, because of its complexity, only a few railwaymen were sufficiently literate to be able to use it. In the early 1840s, however, the electric telegraph was used by some railways to assist in the protection of trains passing through long tunnels. Telegraph operators were stationed at both ends of the tunnel and signalled to each other by spelt-out messages when trains entered and left the tunnel. Gradually the use of the electric telegraph was extended to other sections of line and by 1860 the cumbersome method of transmitting messages letter-by-letter gave place to a simplified version in which an electric current passing through an electro-magnet could hold the single needle deflected to right or left pointing to an indication 'train on line' or 'line clear'.

Here, at last, was an instrument that permitted the replacement of time-interval working by the block system, for the signalmen, as the policemen were now called, could communicate with the men at adjoining stations or junctions. The sections of line between adjacent stations or junctions, termed block sections, formed a space interval between trains, and the block system principle that not more than one train should be allowed on one line in a block section at one time was established, a principle which continues to be the basis of modern signalling today. Single-stroke bells were developed at about the same time so that bell signals could be sent from station to station in conjunction with the block telegraph indications. On some lines, the needle of the telegraph instrument was designed in the shape of a semaphore signal arm, which was horizontal when the line was blocked or lowered at 45 degrees when the line was clear.

The block system was in force throughout the South Eastern Railway main line from London to Dover by 1851 but several years elapsed before it generally superseded time-interval working elsewhere. It may seem strange today that some railways even then did not immediately adopt the new system but some companies still could not afford it while others were sceptical of new-fangled electric devices.

Semaphore Signals Develop

By the 1870s, slotted post semaphore signals had become more-or-less standard on most lines. Distant signals of varying shapes were provided to give drivers advance warning of the indication of a stop signal where sighting was difficult.

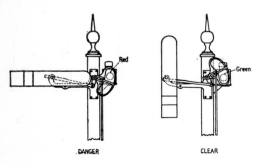

FIG 4 A somersault signal, used on the Great Northern Railway and by other Companies from the late 1870s.

DANGER   CLEAR

Right: A disc and crossbar signal used by several early railways, but particularly the Great Western.

[*Locomotive Publishing Co*

Below right: A selection of Midland Railway arms on a three-way junction near Kentish Town. A miniature lower-quadrant calling-on arm is mounted below the main signals on the right-hand post while the distant arm cn the centre post is fixed at caution.

[*British Railways*

Below: Great Northern Railway somersault signals survived on a number of branches until the 1960s. This one was at Firsby.

[*John Vcughan*

The Abbots Ripton accident on the Great Northern Railway in 1876 resulted in the gradual abandonment of the slotted post type of semaphore signal. This accident occurred during a severe blizzard, and snow and ice had prevented the semaphore arm from returning to danger. Until this time signals were normally maintained in the clear position and were only returned to danger behind a train for the prescribed time-interval, or, where absolute block working was used, until the train cleared the block section ahead. To overcome the possibility of snow falsely holding down a semaphore signal arm, the Great Northern Railway and some other companies standardised a semaphore signal with a balanced arm which was connected through a linkage arrangement to the spectacle casting, in turn pivoted on the outside of the signal post. This type, known as the somersault signal, had only two positions—stop and clear—and lasted from then until the present day, for one or two specimens survive on branch or goods lines. Other companies, too, abandoned the three-position slotted-post semaphore signal but adopted instead a two-position semaphore arm mounted on a simple pivot outside the post, a less complicated type than the somersault signal. Thus appeared the standard lower quadrant signal which we still know today. A white light continued to indicate clear at night, but obviously could be confused with ordinary lighting and, gradually, a green light was adopted for clear, this indication being standardised from 1893. Distant signals with standard semaphore arms, but with a V notch cut out of the left hand end, became established during the 1870s. The arms were painted red to correspond with stop signals and they showed red and white lights at night until the 1890s when they, too, were altered to show red and green.

Despite the introduction of the block telegraph the time-interval system of working lingered on many lines, particularly on double lines. On single lines, it was recognised that the risk of head-on-collision was particularly great and, to facilitate working, many companies installed the block telegraph on single lines before dealing with double-track main lines. To ensure proper working on single lines some companies employed pilotmen to accompany trains on single line sections. As there was only one pilotman to each section and he could only be in one place at one time, there was little risk of collision. When two trains had to pass over the single line in the same direction before one in the reverse direction, the pilotman would instruct the first train to proceed through the section and he would follow on the second train. From this system developed the staff and ticket method of working in which a wooden staff replaced the pilotman. There was only one staff for each section and this had to be carried by or shown to the driver of every train passing through the section. Later, various forms of electrically interlocked staff, token or tablet single line block instrument were developed and have remained the basis of single line operation to the present day. The wooden and electric staff or token systems are described in Chapter 5.

Almost from the start, safety on the railways was supervised by the Board of Trade through the Railway Inspection Department. The Inspecting Officers were (and still are) usually former army officers from the corps of Royal Engineers or the Royal Corps of Transport. New lines of railway had to be inspected and passed by them as being fit for traffic before being opened to the public. The railway companies had to report all accidents to the Board of Trade and, if necessary, an inquiry was held by an Inspecting Officer to ascertain the cause.

The Board of Trade, however, had no power to compel a railway company to adopt improved safety measures and the Inspecting Officers could only recommend action to be taken to prevent a recurrence. Some progressive railways acted on the advice of the Inspecting Officer but others, either by disinclination or by lack of money were loath to introduce additional safety devices.

Interlocking, Brakes and The Block System

The lack of power-operated brakes had led to many collisions because the primitive hand brakes on engines and one or two passenger coaches on each train were inadequate to stop a train at speed quickly. With the time-interval method of signalling, if by chance a train broke down and a second one entered the section, although the driver of the second train might have had a clear view of the first, perhaps half-a-mile ahead, often he could not stop the train in time to avoid a collision. By the 1870s various types of power brake, both automatic and non-automatic, mechanical and pneumatic, were in use although by no means on all railways. A Royal Commission on railway accidents conducted brake trials at Newark in 1875 to ascertain which type of brake provided the best performance. It also recommended the provision of interlocking and signalling by the block telegraph system to be adopted on all lines. The recommendations were endorsed on many occasions by the Inspecting Officers in which the lack of one or other of these features was held to be responsible for accidents. But although most companies were in the process of installing such equipment, it was not until the Regulation of Railways Act, 1889, that they were compelled to adopt the block system, interlocking and automatic continuous brakes. This Act laid the foundations of railway working as we know it today.

Signalling developments during the latter part of the nineteenth century were largely directed towards improvements to existing equipment, often in an endeavour to overcome human error failures. Many were experimental devices— wheel-operated treadles to operate electrical instruments to inform the signalman when a train passed a given point, in some cases developed to provide interlocking with block instruments; forms of automatic train control in which trackside equipment engaged with corresponding equipment on a passing locomotive to give the driver an audible or visual warning of the indication shown by a signal ahead; and power worked signals, operated either by electricity or pneumatically. Many experiments were unsuccessful at that time but some were later improved and adopted. Lock and Block signalling, in which signals could be cleared only when the train ahead had operated treadles on clearing the block section, was one of the systems developed in which the passage of trains governed the actions of a signalman. The system, which remains in use on a few sections of British Railways, is described more fully in a later chapter. The Liverpool Overhead Railway used an automatic semaphore signalling system from its opening in 1893.

The early years of the present century saw the introduction and development of new devices and equipment which form the basis of modern signalling—track circuits, colour-light signals and the automatic control of signals by trains themselves—all of which had been the subject of experiments many years before. The first track circuits had been tried in the 1860s, signals given by coloured lights as early as 1840 and automatic signalling by mechanical contact

FIG 5 A three-position upper quadrant signal installed by a few
railways during and after the first world war.

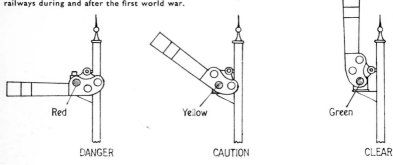

during the 1850s. At that time such devices were not sufficiently reliable to be
used generally. The modern uses of these features are also described later.

Just after the first world war the three-position semaphore signal reappeared
to a limited extent on a few British railways, notably the Great Western and
the South Eastern & Chatham. The signals were based on the American pattern
and worked in the upper quadrant above the horizontal, but to conform with
British practice the arms were on the left of the post. The danger position was
with the arm horizontal and showing a red light at night; caution was displayed
by the arm being raised 45 degrees above horizontal (yellow light at night) and
clear by the arm in the vertical position (green light at night). To avoid
confusion with the standard two-position semaphore signals which worked in
the lower quadrant the three-position signals of necessity had to work in the
upper quadrant. When at caution, the next signal was at danger.

These signals used a yellow light for caution, although normal two-position
distant signals still used red for their caution (still at that time termed danger)
position. Admittedly some companies distinguished their distant signals by
additional indications such as that given by the Coligny Welch signal lamp in
which a white > was illuminated at night alongside the colour indication.
Otherwise a driver relied entirely on his knowledge of the road to know whether
he was approaching a stop or distant signal. The three-position signal installations although not extensive led to considerable controversy among signal
engineers as to the desirability of generally adopting three-position signalling
again.

The more conservative of the signal engineers preferred to retain the red light
in a distant as a definite stop indication, feeling that caution did not lay sufficient
emphasis on stop at the next signal. Others felt that signal aspects should be
clarified. Although in this country the three-position semaphore simply gave
an indication of the next signal ahead, the three-position signal in America
was used as a speed signal. In this system the signal aspects indicated at what
speed a train should run on passing through a junction rather than to indicate

Above: The impressive gantry south of Rugby in LNWR days. The miniature arms on the lower gantry merely repeated the indications of the main arms above. Note the distant arms painted in a similar manner to the stop arms and the ringed home and distant arms applying here to the down slow line.   [*British Railways*

Below: The simplification of aspects brought about by the introduction of colour-light signals is illustrated in this later view of Rugby showing the three four-aspect colour-light signals which replaced the entire gantry shown above. These signals in fact provided more indications than the semaphores above.   [*British Railways*

the route it was to take and leave the speed regulation to the driver's judgment. Additional aspects were obtained by mounting two three-position arms on the same post. Also, the Metropolitan and District railways in London had adopted two-position yellow distant arms with a yellow light for caution.

In view of the problems raised by the introduction of yellow for caution and by the very use of a three-position signal as a speed signal, the Institution of Railway Signal Engineers set up in 1922 a committee to investigate the whole matter of three-position signalling.

The committee's report produced in 1924 recommended against the adoption of three-position semaphore signalling but were in favour of three-aspect colour-light signalling with red as the danger aspect, yellow for caution, green for clear. In fact, they suggested the use of a fourth aspect on lines carrying a heavy service of suburban and express trains: double-yellow—attention, run at medium speed. The committee also recommended the substitution of yellow for red in semaphore distant signals at danger (caution). The Ministry of Transport (which had taken over on its formation in 1919, the railway supervisory functions from the Board of Trade) endorsed the committee's findings and ordained that semaphore distant signals should be painted yellow instead of red and display yellow and green lights at night. The recommendation against the adoption of the three-position semaphore signal left the way open for the introduction of the upper quadrant two-position semaphore signal, since there was now no possibility of confusion between three- and two-position signals in the upper quadrant.

The 1924 recommendations were so far reaching that there has been no need for any major alteration in signalling aspects either in semaphore or colour light practice since their adoption 50 years ago, and they will undoubtedly remain so long as there is a need for lineside visual signals. Today, railway safety comes under the scrutiny of the Department of the Environment.

Below left: Three-position upper-quadrant semaphore signals were not employed widely in Britain. The Great Central installed a few in the Scunthorpe area which lasted until the late 1960s. This example is shown in the vertical, clear position.   [*British Railways*
Below right: The Western Region of BR followed GWR practice and continued to use lower quadrant signals in sempahore areas. This gantry has metal arms on tubular steel posts.

2—Types of Signal—Semaphore
(See diagrams on pages 49, 50 and 51)

The semaphore signal consists of a wood or metal arm, 4-5ft long, and 9in-1ft deep, mounted at the top and to the left of a wood, metal or concrete post varying in height to suit local sighting requirements. Attached to the right hand end of the arm as viewed from the front are the coloured glass spectacles; by night a lamp, usually oil but occasionally electric, illuminates these spectacles from behind and gives the colour indications. Semaphore signals have two positions—when the arm is in the horizontal position it is at danger, and when inclined downwards or upwards at between 45 and 60 degrees from horizontal it is clear. As strict safety regulations require the arm to return to the horizontal position if a failure occurs, a heavy spectacle casting and balance weight had to be fitted to lower quadrant signals to ensure that the arm moved upwards to the danger position. The upper quadrant arm, which is inclined upwards in the clear position, drops by gravity to danger and much of the balancing equipment is unnecessary. For the past 40 years or so lower quadrant arms have gradually been replaced with upper quadrants as renewals have become due. However, there are still many lower quadrant signals in use; the Great Western Railway, and its successor, the Western Region of British Railways, has resisted any such change, and lower quadrant signals are still in universal use on its lines retaining mechanical signalling. They are also found elsewhere to a small extent on other parts of British Railways but are rapidly becoming extinct.

Running Signals

Running signals are those signals which control and protect through running movements on running lines as distinct from sidings. There are two types of running signal—stop and distant.

The Stop Signal

A semaphore stop signal, whether upper or lower quadrant, consists of a rectangular arm. The side facing oncoming trains is painted red with a broad white vertical stripe near the outer, left hand end, while on the back it is painted white with a black vertical stripe in a similar position. At night the glass spectacles show a red light when the arm is in the horizontal danger or on position, and a green light when the arm is in the inclined clear or off position.

A stop signal may not be passed at danger except in cases of failure or where authorised. The function of stop signals is to divide the line into sections so that trains on the same line run at an adequate distance from each other. They are installed at the entrance to all block sections, and at the approach to junctions and points to afford them protection. At diverging junctions a separate stop signal is provided for each alternative route, and thus the driver of an approaching train is informed which route is set up, in addition to the state of the line ahead. On all junction signals, the primary or high speed route is indicated by the arm on the highest post; the arms for diverging routes are placed on lower posts to the right or left of the main post, according to the

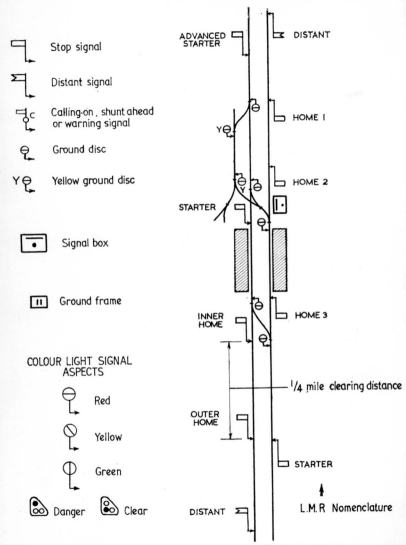

FIG 6 Key to the signalling diagrams in this publication.

FIG 7 Signalling layout, including nomenclature, at a typical double-track station.

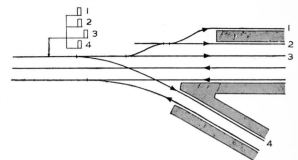

FIG 8 Semaphore junction signals usually have a separate arm for each route.

direction of the divergence. At complicated junctions, where speeds are often low, junction or splitting stop signals are sometimes replaced by a single arm with a route indicator which exhibits stencil letter or number codes corresponding to the official designation of each of the routes. The signalman must still pull the lever for the appropriate route, and each time the same arm clears, but with a different code exhibited in the indicator according to the route set. When the signal is at danger, the indicator does not show a route code. When trains are to be diverted from a main line to a lower speed route as an out-of-course working, the junction signal is normally held at danger until the train is closely approaching it.

Stop signals are themselves divided into two types: home signals, usually placed on the approach side of a signal box, and starting signals, placed beyond or in advance of a signalbox. In railway parlance the terms 'in advance' or 'rear' have definite meanings. These can be visualised easily by imagining a person standing on a line facing the direction towards which trains normally run on that line. Everything in front of him is said to be in advance, everything behind him is in rear. Thus a train standing at a home signal is in the rear of or outside the signal. When it has passed the home signal it is in advance of or inside the signal. Wherever junctions, crossovers or yard exits occur, additional signals are necessary to provide adequate protection and to prevent any conflicting movements over crossovers or through junctions; in addition, extra home signals are often provided for acceptance purposes. Before a signalman can accept a train from the previous signalbox, the line must usually be clear for ¼-mile beyond his home signal; this ¼-mile overlap is provided in case a driver should misjudge his brake application, fail to bring the train under proper

FIG 9 Diagram explaining the terms "in rear of" and "in advance of" in railway parlance.

◄—— IN REAR OF X   POINT X   IN ADVANCE OF X ——►

DIRECTION OF TRAVEL ——►

Above: Examples of lower quadrant stop signals, with, on the left, a North Eastern slotted-post signal and, on the right, an under-slung bracket junction signal on the SR.   [*S. Creer; J. Scrace*
Below: Examples of lower quadrant stop and distant signals on the same post. On the left is a **Great** Central type with wooden arms, on the right an SR (LBSCR) signal mounted on a concrete post.   [*T, G. Flinders; G. M. Kichenside*

control in time, and pass the signal at danger. It is, in effect, a safety margin. The end of the ¼-mile overlap is known as the clearing point. It is not always possible to keep a ¼-mile clear beyond the home signal for any length of time, especially at busy junctions, or where crossovers between running lines occur, so a second stop signal, known as an outer home, is often provided a ¼-mile on the approach side of what is now the inner home to give the required clearance.

Small signal boxes without crossovers or junctions may have only one stop signal, a home, for each direction; others may have as many as four or even more in each direction—an outer home, an inner home, a starter and an advanced starter. This nomenclature of signals is standard on British Railways, although the London Midland Region classifies all stop signals as home, irrespective of their position in relation to the signalbox, except the stop signal which governs entry into the block section ahead, which is known as the starter. In addition, the terms inner, outer and advanced are dispensed with and all signals are known as home No 1, home No 2 etc (in the order in which trains normally approach them) and starter.

Where signalboxes are very close together one signal may be worked from both boxes, perhaps as starter for one and home for the other. In this case the arm is worked through a slotting device on the post. Both signalmen must pull the appropriate levers for the signal to clear. (See page 34.)

The Distant Signal

The distant arm is the same length and width as a stop arm, but has a vee notch cut out of the outer, left hand end. The approach side is painted yellow and has a black vee stripe near the left hand end corresponding to the vee notch. The back of the arm is white with a black vee stripe in a similar position. By night, the glass spectacles show a yellow light in the caution or on position, and green in the clear or off position. A distant signal indicates caution, and may be passed in the on position. The function of a distant signal is to give the driver of an approaching train prior warning of the indication of the stop signals ahead. A distant signal is sited about ½-¾ mile before the first of the stop signals to which it applies, the distance depending on the gradient and maximum

FIG 10 Where signal boxes are close together, the distant signal worked by one box may be placed on the same post below one or more of the stop signals at the previous box.

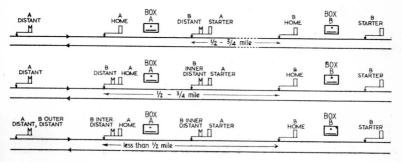

Four types of upper quadrant signal: *above left* are two standard LNER signals mounted on concrete posts. Note the indications of the lower stop arms repeated by co-acting arms at the tops of the posts. *Above right* is a former LSW gantry with SR upper quadrant arms and three-aspect colour-light distant signals. *Below left* is an LMS distant signal and *below right* is a detail rear view of two slotted stop and distant arms. [J. C. Flemins, British Railways, Alan Williams

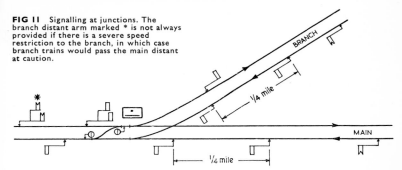

FIG 11 Signalling at junctions. The branch distant arm marked * is not always provided if there is a severe speed restriction to the branch, in which case branch trains would pass the main distant at caution.

line speed. A distant signal can only be cleared to the off position when all the stop signals to which it applies on the line ahead worked from the same signalbox have also been cleared. Similarly, none of the stop signals can be returned to danger until the distant signal has first been replaced to caution. This is achieved by interlocking, explained in more detail in Chapter 4. In order to maintain the ¾-mile braking distance, where signalboxes are close together, it is often necessary to have the distant signal for one box mounted under the starting signal of the previous signalbox in the rear. In this case, a slotting device is provided on the signal post which prevents the distant arm showing clear if the stop signal above it is at danger.

If the boxes are so close that two distant signals are required, one each beneath the starter and the advanced starter, or home and starting signals of the previous box, they are known as outer and inner distants respectively. At the approaches to diverging junctions which may be negotiated at moderate or high speed, splitting distant signals are often provided with a separate distant arm repeating each of the splitting home signals. At other junctions, where only a single distant is provided, it is cleared only for the main line, and remains at caution when the branch route is cleared. On some single line branches at the approach to passing loops, or occasionally on main lines where permanent speed restrictions exist, fixed distant signals are provided. These are unworked distant arms, permanently set at caution.

Subsidiary Signals

Subsidiary signals control low speed shunting and other non-running movements, both on main lines and in yards. In pre-grouping days there was less uniformity between companies in the design and use of subsidiary signals and

FIG 12 A track layout showing the placing of a yellow shunting disc and a shunt ahead subsidiary arm.

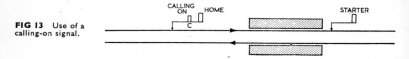

FIG 13 Use of a
calling-on signal.

there were several alternative types of arm with the same meaning. Some companies evolved individual types of arms for specific movements. The Great Western Railway, for example, had a special backing signal for wrong direction running within station limits, consisting of a miniature red arm with two holes side by side in the face of the arm.

For shunting movements on running lines in the same direction as the normal flow of through traffic, the subsidiary signal often takes the form of a miniature upper or lower quadrant arm mounted below the main running stop signal. Shunt-ahead, calling-on and warning signals come into this category. The shunt-ahead arm is usually placed under a starting signal to allow a train to draw forward into the block section ahead, before reversing over trailing points into a siding or loop.

The calling-on arm, on the other hand, is usually placed under a home signal, and allows the driver of a second train to proceed into an occupied platform as far as the line is clear. This allows additional vehicles to be attached to the rear of standing trains.

The warning signal is used only in specially authorised locations in conjunction with the warning arrangement, explained in Chapter 5. The calling-on, shunt-ahead and warning signals consist of miniature red arms which carry the letters C, S and W respectively. The latest pattern upper quadrant signals of this type consist of a miniature red arm with a white horizontal stripe. When pulled

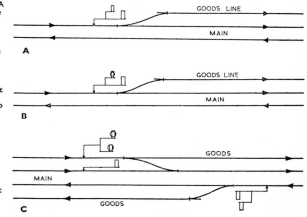

FIG 14 Example A shows the entrance to a goods line controlled by a miniature semaphore arm bracketed from the main post, as used on the London Midland Region. Example B shows the same layout but the signal controlling entry to the goods line is a ringed semaphore as used in many places on the Southern Region. Example C shows the Western Region use of a ringed semaphore on goods lines, including movement from a goods line to a main line.

Subsidiary shunting signals: *above left* is a Midland type, *above* the LNWR variation. *Centre left* the standard SR mechanical disc and, *below left*, LNW revolving discs. *Below* is a standard Southern Region banner repeater signal.   [*British Railways* (3); *Alan Williams* (2)

off, these signals reveal an illuminated letter C, S or W. At night, these signals show a miniature red or white light in the on position, and green in the off position.

The semaphore arm with a superimposed ring near its left-hand end, although common in pre-grouping days, is now confined to the Southern and Western Regions. The Southern uses it as a main line signal governing entry to yards or goods lines. The Western uses it on goods lines or as a yard exit signal. Ringed arms are however obsolete and will be replaced by more modern types of signal.

Ground signals control shunting movements over crossovers which are normally trailing to the general direction of traffic, or through connections between running lines and yards. Just as the shunt ahead signal is used to allow trains to draw forward beyond a trailing crossover, so a ground signal would control the actual reversing movement. Ground signals are also employed to protect the exits from little-used sidings where the provision of a full size stop signal is not warranted. The old-type ground signals, many of which are still in use today, consist of miniature semaphore arms and are painted in a similar manner to full size semaphore signals, with red arms and a vertical white stripe. The modern equivalent to these signals is the white metal disc with a horizontal red stripe. A similar disc, black with a yellow horizontal stripe, is not a repeater or distant signal, but is a stop signal in its own right. It is only cleared when the route is set for a diverging movement over a crossover from a siding or yard to a running line. It may, however, be passed in the on position when the points to which it applies are set straight ahead towards a siding or headshunt. In such a case a train can shunt backwards and forwards quite freely into the headshunt with the signal at danger. Very often, where there are several alternative routes in a yard or leading from the yard, several subsidiary shunting or ground signals are required, one for each route. It is not always possible to mount these signals on gantries, as with running junction signals, and up to five miniature arms or discs may be mounted one above another. In such a case the arms read in descending order from left to right, the top arm applying to the extreme left hand divergence, and the lowest arm to the extreme right hand divergence.

Repeater Signals

Where signals would be difficult to see, perhaps because of an intervening bridge or overhanging station roof, special measures may be necessary to ensure that a driver has a clear view of them to act in accordance with their indication in sufficient time. In some cases, what are known as co-acting arms are provided on the same signal post, one arm high up, with a sky background, giving the driver a long range view of the signal, the other arm low down, more-or-less at driver's eye level but, perhaps, out of sight until the train approaches to within 50-100yd or less. The lower arm may be necessary for a close view of the signal to prevent the driver from having to lean well out of the cab in order to see the sky arm, perhaps, when restarting from a station stop. Co-acting arms, which are usually mounted at the extremities of the post, should not be confused with the somewhat rare splitting junction signal, in which because of confined location the arms are mounted one above the other.

Elsewhere, banner repeater signals may be employed. These consist of a rectangular black arm (with a vee notch cut from the left hand end in the case of distant signal repeaters) mounted in a circular glass-fronted frame and with an opaque white background behind it. The arm is horizontal when the signal to which it applies is at danger, and inclined at 45 degrees, up or down usually depending on whether the main signal is upper or lower quadrant, for clear. Banner signals are placed about 50-200yd to the rear of the signal they repeat, depending on location. In a few places, in confined locations red-arm banner signals may be used as stop signals in their own right and function exactly as normal semaphore stop signals.

3—Types of Signal—Colour-Light
(See diagrams on pages 52 and 53)

Running Signals

Although semaphore signalling remains in use on many lines in Britain, most heavily-trafficked trunk or suburban routes have been either partially or completely resignalled with colour-light signals. The initial cost of installation of colour-light signals is high, but otherwise they have many advantages. Unlike semaphores, they show the same indications by day and by night; their powerful beams penetrate all but the thickest of fogs; their shape and size makes them much easier to place at driver's eye level, and in the multiple-lens type of colour-light signal, there are no moving mechanical parts. Moreover, the indications are simpler than those exhibited by semaphore signals. On long sections of main line, colour-light signals may be operated by the passage of the trains themselves by track circuits, and thus many intermediate signal-boxes may be abolished.

There are two types of colour light signal—the searchlight signal and the multi-lens signal. A searchlight signal has a single lamp and lens; the operation of a sliding spectacle plate with appropriately coloured glasses between the lamp and the lens of the signal determines which aspect is displayed. The multi-lens signal is more common, however, and has a separate lamp and lens for each aspect. Usually they are mounted one above the other, but in a few early installations cluster four-aspect signals were installed. They had their four aspects mounted diamond-wise on a circular head; the yellow lenses are mounted at the top and bottom, the red to the right and the green to the left. Although of different construction, both searchlight and multi-lens signals display similar indications.

The earliest and simplest forms of colour-light signal showed only two aspects —red and green for stop signals and yellow and green for distant signals. These signals are merely colour-light versions of the semaphore signal, and are used where isolated colour-light signals have replaced semaphores, particularly in the case of distant signals. On high speed main lines of the former LMS and LNER, two-aspect colour-light distant signals were introduced extensively in replacement of semaphore signals. For the signalman there is the advantage that they do not require a heavy pull on the lever (a mechanical semaphore distant signal, perhaps 1200yd from the box, requires considerable manual effort to operate it), and the driver of the train has a distinctive, powerful signal

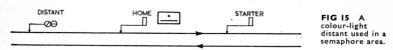

FIG 15 A colour-light distant used in a semaphore area.

which can be seen clearly even in the worst weather. Some of the LM colour-light distants have three lenses. They are not three-aspect signals and the third lens is merely a second yellow light which is illuminated only if the main yellow caution aspect fails. In most modern colour-light signals double filament bulbs are used so that if one filament burns out, the second filament is automatically brought into use to prevent a signal failure.

Isolated colour-light signals have also been installed to replace semaphore stop signals, but this practice has been limited to only a few locations in what are nominally semaphore areas. One problem in such cases has been to ensure that there is no confusion of aspects shown by isolated colour-light stop signals. In colour-light areas, a multiple-aspect signal cannot display a green—clear indication unless the next signal is showing at least a caution if not a clear aspect also. In normal working, therefore, a multiple-aspect signal at green cannot be followed by the next signal ahead showing red. But in a nominally semaphore area, if a semaphore home signal were to be replaced by a two-aspect (red/green) colour-light signal showing exactly the same colour indications, the powerful green aspect might lead a driver into thinking that the next signal (the starting signal) is also clear when, in semaphore practice, this is not necessarily the case. If a home signal is converted to a colour-light it must be renewed as a three-aspect signal. There is, of course, no reason why the most advanced starting signal of a box should not be a two-aspect colour-light, for it is followed by a distant signal for the box ahead, so that this problem does not arise.

Three-aspect signals show red, yellow or green indications, corresponding to the night-time red and yellow, green and yellow or double green indications of a semaphore stop signal with a distant beneath it. There is no corresponding semaphore indication to the colour-light double-yellow indication, explained later. In colour-light areas, where every signal shows three- or four-aspects, except in some of the earlier installations confined solely to a station area, the terms distant, home and starting do not apply, for every multiple-aspect signal serves as a distant, home and starting signal at the same time. Block working from signal box to signal box, with block sections between, as used in semaphore signalling, may be abolished where colour-light signals are installed and

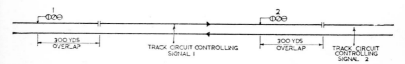

FIG 16 The basic layout of the track circuit control of colour-light signals.

The first four-aspect colour-light signals in Britain were brought into use in 1926 on the SR for electrification. At that time simple running junctions had a separate signal head for each route.
[*British Railways*

A Southern Region three-aspect signal at Waterloo, with the signal showing yellow, and the theatre type route indicator illuminated. Note also the floodlit shunting disc signal.
[*Alan Williams*

provided the line is equipped with continuous track circuiting. Instead, the distance between each colour-light signal becomes, in effect, the block section. Each signal has a suitable overlap to allow for braking errors to correspond with the $\frac{1}{4}$-mile clearing distance beyond semaphore home signals. The distance, however, is not always as much as a $\frac{1}{4}$-mile; on many lines with four-aspect signals the overlap is normally about 200yd or about ten coach lengths, and it may be as little as 60ft, or one coach length, in some low-speed areas.

Colour-light signals are spaced as evenly as possible to allow the maximum uninterrupted flow of traffic. Even with three-aspect signalling, however, there is a limitation on the spacing of signals since each signal, besides being a stop signal, is also a distant signal for the next signal ahead. It must therefore be at least about $\frac{3}{4}$-mile from the signals ahead and in the rear, so that an adequate braking distance is maintained. This means that trains on the same line must run at least two miles apart if the second train is not to be checked by a yellow caution aspect behind the first train. Four-aspect signals may be placed at closer intervals because their double-yellow preliminary caution aspect provides braking distance over two signal sections. Locomotive-hauled trains can begin to brake at the double-yellow signal, but gain further advice on the state of the line ahead at the next signal, while diesel and electric multiple-unit trains which may have more powerful brakes, can proceed at speed up to the signal showing a single-yellow aspect and commence their brake application there. Trains running at 100/125 mph, though, normally need at least 2,200 yds braking distance.

The four-aspect signal has, reading from bottom to top, red, yellow, green and yellow lenses, and shows red, single yellow (the bottom one only of the two), double yellow (both) and green. The two yellow lenses are separated by the green lens, and this arrangement splits the two yellow beams of the double-yellow indication, and ensures that there is no confusion between yellow and double yellow aspects. On searchlight signals, a second lens, showing yellow or nothing, is added to a normal three-aspect searchlight signal head, permitting the display of the double-yellow indication. Although some of the first four-aspect colour-light signals used on the LMS, LNER and SR had the second yellow aspect mounted below the red lens, with the green lens at the top, this arrangement is now obsolete, and these signals are gradually being replaced with heads incorporating the standard arrangement given above.

On most modern signals, the red lens is the lowest aspect; this arrangement permits the danger indication to be placed at driver's eye level, yet allows all aspects to be mounted at a sufficient height to be observed at a distance. An added advantage is that there is no lens hood below the red lens on which falling snow could build up and obscure the light. Four- and three-aspect signals are not normally used together, since this would entail uneven spacing of signals, but four-aspect signals are sometimes used in a predominantly three-aspect area at the approach to stations or junctions, when two adjacent signals are, of necessity, closer than the normal minimum allowed for three-aspect signals.

Unlike semaphore signals, colour-light junction signals do not normally have a separate signal for each diverging route. Instead, a single signal is employed, with, above it, a junction indicator. On running lines this indicator usually takes the form of a series of three or five white lights aligned at 45 degrees to the left or right, according to the direction of the divergence. These white or

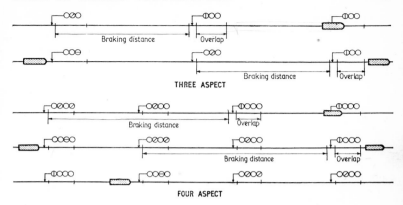

THREE ASPECT

FOUR ASPECT

FIG 17 Diagrams illustrating the spacing and aspects shown by three- and four-aspect signals.

lunar lights are illuminated only when the diverging route is set up, and are extinguished when the signal is at danger, or when the main route is set up. If the signal controls more than one diverging route to the left or right, additional rows of lights at 90 and 135 degrees are provided, as shown in Fig 18. At the approach to large through or terminal stations, where trains approach at low speeds, one signal might lead to up to a dozen or more diverging routes. In this case, a direction indicator would not be suitable, and instead a theatre-type indicator, showing the platform or line number, or letter designation, is provided. In this case the letters or numbers are formed with lamps, and an indication is given for every route. No indication is displayed when the signal is at danger.

In some of the older installations, particularly those with the non-standard four-aspect signals noted above, a separate colour-light signal might be provided for each route, contrary to standard practice.

Distant indications for diverging routes are not now normally provided in colour-light areas. Occasionally, however, at the approach to certain diverging

FIG 18 Colour-light signalling at junctions. When the route is set for the un-numbered track, the route indicator above the signal will not be illuminated. The SR three-light route indicator is being replaced by the standard five-light type.

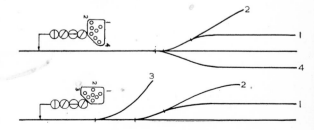

junctions, separate distant multiple-aspect signals are provided. Only the main signal aspect shows danger, and caution is indicated by both signals showing yellow alongside each other. This indication should not be confused with the double yellow, preliminary caution, indication of four-aspect signals, which is shown vertically. Clear is shown only by the signal applicable to the route which has been set up; the adjacent signal continues to display a single yellow.

At most facing junctions, a moderate speed restriction is enforced over the diverging route, and in this case there is no advance indication at the preceding signal of the diversion. Usually, the signal circuits are so arranged that when the junction is set for the diverging route, the signal preceding the junction signal displays only a single yellow aspect and the junction signal itself is approach controlled. In this case the junction signal remains at danger, even though the route has been set up and the appropriate signal lever or route switch cleared in the signalbox. Only when the approaching train has passed the preceding signal at caution and occupied the approach, or berth track circuit, will the junction signal clear for the train, the timing of the release mechanism depending on the severity of the speed restriction through the junction. At high speed junctions, for example Weaver Junction on the West Coast main line where the Liverpool line leaves the Euston—Glasgow route, and where the speed restriction over the diverging route may be 70mph compared with 90mph on the straight route, trains for the diverging track are checked by a double yellow indication at the second signal before the junction. Medium speed junctions (50-60mph for 100mph main routes) are more of a problem since normal approach control by a single yellow at the signal before the junction signal might be too restrictive if the junction signal cannot be seen well ahead. Thus at Hanslope Junction between Bletchley and Rugby for trains crossing between fast and slow lines the signal beyond the junction is held at danger until the train is closely approaching the junction signal itself at yellow, which if the line ahead is clear changes to green just before the train passes. At certain junctions flashing yellow aspects are displayed at the signals preceding the junction signal. (See page 124).

At converging junctions, normal multiple-aspect signals protect the junction much as home signals do in semaphore areas. Depending on the type of train involved, the usual approach speeds of trains, and the proximity of the signal to the conflicting junction, trains may either be held at the preceding signal, or in low speed areas they may be allowed up to the signal immediately protecting the junction, even though a conflicting move is taking place just ahead.

At the approach to a colour-light area, the preceding semaphore signal often carries a two- (yellow or green) or three-aspect (yellow, double-yellow or green) colour light distant; this signal is unlit when the semaphore arm above it is at danger, but shows the appropriate aspects with the arm at clear.

At the termination of a colour-light area, the last four-aspect signal may well be followed by a three-aspect signal, and finally a two-aspect stop signal, with the semaphore distant for the next signal box ahead beyond it. This arrangement, however, requires the last two signals to be spaced at least ¾-mile apart, to allow an adequate braking distance. More often, the three-aspect signal is also employed as the inner distant for the semaphore stop signals ahead, the previous four-aspect signal providing the outer distant (double-yellow) indication when

Above: Standard LMR four-aspect colour-light signal gantry on multi-track routes with overhead catenary electrification.
Below left: WR four-aspect colour-light signal with three-way junction indicator for routes diverging to the right of the main route.   [*British Railways*

Right: LMR three-aspect signal with theatre-type route indicator, position-light shunt signal, right-away signal (R) and telephone.
                    [*British Railways*

Below: A position-light shunt signal in the clear position with the stencil route indicator illuminated.
                    [*British Railways*

appropriate. Thus the distance between the last colour-light and the first semaphore signals may be considerably reduced.

Subsidiary and Shunting Signals

The design of subsidiary and shunting signals employed in colour-light areas varies from area to area, and even from place to place within an area, but the indications they display are nevertheless standardised. Subsidiary signals are normally placed on the same post and under a main signal. Shunt signals normally stand on their own. There are several types of shunt signal; some are miniature colour-light signals with smaller lenses which display the same red, yellow or green indications of the running signals. These signals may be compared to the miniature arms used for subsidiary movements in semaphore areas. The position-light shunt signal has three miniature lights arranged in a triangle; the bottom left hand light shows a red light, and the other two white lights. When in the on position, the bottom red and the right-hand white light are displayed; when cleared, the red light is extinguished and the second white light, mounted above the red lens, is illuminated. In the case of the shunting signal which may be passed at danger, the red lens may be replaced by a yellow light. Some shunt signals are unlit when on, but show two white lights at a 45 degree angle when cleared to denote correct detection of hand points. In the latest power signalling schemes a draw-ahead subsidiary signal is employed for authorising a driver to pass a main signal at danger for shunting. The proceed aspect is given by two white lights at 45deg like the position-light shunt signal. If it is accompanied by a route indication it allows a train to proceed towards the next signal or towards buffer stops, but the driver must be prepared to stop short of any obstruction. Without a route indication when clear the signal allows a train to proceed past for shunting. Any movement past a draw-ahead signal must not pass any other signal at danger.

Semaphore type discs, but fitted with electric motors, and floodlit at night, are also used. As yellow tends to merge with white at a distance the shunting signals which may be passed when on are black, with a horizontal yellow band. Calling-on and shunt ahead signals in colour-light areas may be either a position-light signal, sometimes with an illuminated letter C or S when cleared, or they may be floodlit discs, with two thin, parallel horizontal red lines with a red letter C or S on the face of the disc. The warning signal is not normally used in colour-light areas, and there is, therefore, no equivalent to this signal on the colour-light scene. Instead, if the overlap beyond a signal is partially infringed by a conflicting movement, at some places the next signal in the rear may clear to a yellow aspect only after an approaching train has operated a time release to ensure that the train's speed has been sufficiently reduced.

In some places, where facing points gives access to a siding, yard or loop a single-aspect subsidiary colour-light signal may be used. Normally, no light is displayed, but when cleared, a miniature yellow aspect is illuminated, the main signal above remaining at danger. In new installations a position-light subsidiary is used for the same purpose.

Semaphore-type banner repeater signals are also used where necessary in colour-light areas. The banner signal arm is horizontal when the colour-light signal it repeats is at danger and inclined at 45 degrees for other aspects.

4—Allied Safety Devices

All signals, points and facing point locks in every signalbox, both mechanical and electric, are interlocked to prevent a signalman setting up two conflicting routes at the same time and to ensure that signals can be cleared only when the points to which they apply are correctly set, thus removing as far as possible the risk of collision or derailment. In manual signalboxes, interlocking is achieved by tappets and rods mounted beneath the lever frame in the locking room, usually on the ground floor. Obviously, no two signalboxes control exactly the same layout of points and signals, so every locking frame must be specially designed and assembled. Locking must prevent all possible combinations of lever movements which will set up conflicting routes, but must at the same time permit non-conflicting parallel movements to be made.

In large signalboxes, the locking is very complicated. Fig 19 shows a double line with a cross-over and distant, home and starting signals in one direction. Also shown is part of the locking for this particular layout. The frame is shown in the normal position with all signals on, and the crossover normal for through running. To signal a train, the signalman must first pull lever 2, the home signal. The tappet of lever 2 then slides down so that opening X is opposite pin C. It also, by virtue of its shape, forces pin A and locking bar M to the left. This brings pin E into aperture V, and prevents the crossover lever 4 from being reversed with the protecting home signal cleared. Next the signalman pulls the starting signal lever 3; this brings tappet 3 down, with aperture Y down opposite pin D. Now, with pins C and D opposite apertures X and Y, the distant lever 1 may be pulled. This action brings pin B out of aperture Z, forces locking bar N

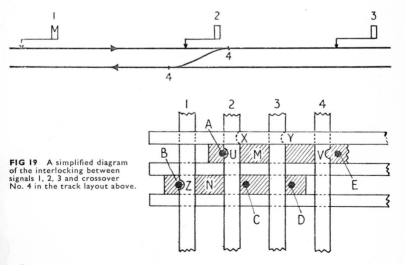

FIG 19 A simplified diagram of the interlocking between signals 1, 2, 3 and crossover No. 4 in the track layout above.

C

to the left and locks C and D in apertures X and Y, which prevents the home and starting signal levers 2 and 3 being returned to danger until the distant lever 1 has first been returned to caution.

If crossover 4 is reversed, locking bar M is prevented from sliding to the left by pin E, and thus home signal 2 cannot be cleared and this in turn locks distant signal 1 at caution. The interlocking allows starter 3 to be cleared because it is beyond the crossover, and may be required to start a movement originating from across the crossover.

Locking in some electric and electro-mechanical boxes is achieved by electric locks in which mechanical lock bolts are electrically worked. In the latest BR power installations interlocking is achieved in the electric circuits by relays. This is more compact but the wiring is very complicated. All interlocking must be made to fail safe. In other words, if an electric lock, relay or circuit fails for any reason, it must lock associated equipment so that signals concerned go to danger until the lineman finds and rectifies the fault. An important safety feature found in modern electrical installations is the time release circuit which incorporates a thermal relay. Its most common application is to colour-light signalling installations. If a signalman wants to cancel a route he has set up, he replaces the signals to danger manually (as opposed to the train doing so automatically). The time release mechanism then comes into operation and prevents any conflicting movement from being set up for a stipulated period, usually about two minutes. This time interval is sufficient to allow any train which might have been closely approaching the signal, unobserved by the signalman, to come to a stand, and any risk of collision because of a train over-running a signal returned to danger in front of it is thus averted. Another use of a time release is in the approach control of a signal as we saw in the last chapter, although in these cases the time of the release varies and depends on the length of the approach track circuit and the speed restriction through the junction.

Slotting

Not all locking is done in the signalbox, however. In semaphore areas when the distant signal for one box is mounted beneath the starter of the box in rear,

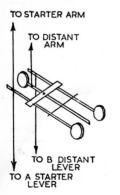
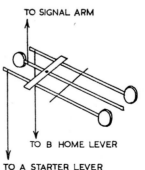

TO STARTER ARM

TO DISTANT ARM

TO SIGNAL ARM

TO B DISTANT LEVER

TO A STARTER LEVER

TO B HOME LEVER

TO A STARTER LEVER

FIG 20 Diagrams illustrating the method of slotting signals. On the left is the arrangement for a stop and distant signal on the same post; on the right is the arrangement for a stop signal controlled from two boxes.

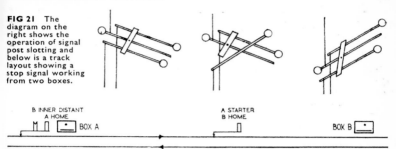

FIG 21 The diagram on the right shows the operation of signal post slotting and below is a track layout showing a stop signal working from two boxes.

B INNER DISTANT
A HOME

BOX A

A STARTER
B HOME

BOX B

locking has to be provided on the post to ensure that the distant can only be cleared when the stop signal above it has also been cleared, and also that the distant will return to caution when the stop signal above is returned to danger. This is achieved by means of balance weights and a slot bar, and is known as slotting. The principle is illustrated in Figs 20 and 21.

Facing Point Locks

Department of the Environment regulations require every facing point on running lines used by passenger trains to be equipped with facing point locks. Simply, a facing point lock consists of a bar with two holes into which a bolt fits. The bar forms part of the stretcher bar between the point blades. The bolt is connected via rodding to a locking lever in the signalbox. Thus, before a signalman can reverse a set of facing points, he must restore the locking lever, which withdraws the bolt from one of the holes. He then reverses the points and reverses the point lock lever; the bolt is inserted in the other hole and locks the points in the reverse position. The facing point lock lever is interlocked so that none of the signals protecting the points can be cleared until the points are set and locked one way or the other. The locking on the actual point lever ensures that only the correct signals can be cleared. Locking levers normally stand reversed in the frame when the points are locked.

Detection

As an additional safety measure, all facing points and some trailing, over which running movements are made are detected to ensure that the point blades are fully home and have correctly obeyed the lever movement. This is achieved mechanically or electrically. The mechanical detector illustrated in Fig 22 comprises interlocking slides connected to the point blades and signal operating wires respectively and so arranged that the signal wire slide becomes free only when the blades are correctly and fully set for the route it controls. Where one signal arm applies to a route in which there are several facing points the signal wire is taken through detectors at every set of points concerned on its way from the signal lever to the signal itself. The lie of mechanical points is sometimes detected electrically, and repeated on an indicator in the signalbox. Power operated points are electrically detected and must be proved set in the correct position before the signal operating circuits can function.

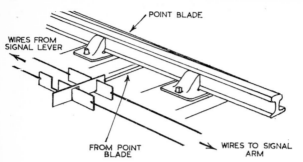

POINT BLADE

WIRES FROM
SIGNAL LEVER

FROM POINT
BLADE

WIRES TO SIGNAL
ARM

FIG 22 Simplified diagram showing the detection between signals and facing points. In practice there are generally three slides from the points—one from each blade and one from the facing point lock. All must be in their correct position for the signal slide to pass freely.

Fouling Bars

To make sure that the point blades are not moved under a train, some mechanically-worked facing points are equipped with a fouling bar, which lies along the inside edge of the running rails, and is connected to the point lock. The act of withdrawing the facing point lock bolt raises the fouling bar into the flangeway. If a train were passing, the fouling bar would be prevented from rising by the wheel flanges of the train, and thus it would be impossible for the bolt to be withdrawn and the point blades to be moved. In all power installations and on most mechanically-worked facing points, a track circuit through the points is used instead of a fouling bar, to serve the same purpose.

Sequential Locking

Interlocking is not used only to prevent conflicting routes being set up and to prove points and signals are correctly set; it can also be used to ensure that one train is not inadvertently signalled into the back of another. This application is known as sequential locking, and has been installed at many boxes on main lines where semaphore signalling is used. The locking permits the running signals to be pulled only in a certain order, say the outer home, inner home, starter, advanced starter and finally the distant. The locking is arranged so that a stop signal cannot be cleared unless the next signal ahead worked by the same box is at danger. Thus the signals cannot be cleared for a second train unless they have been returned to danger behind the first. It will be seen that, if employed in conjunction with track circuits, this method all but eliminates the risk of collision from a signalman's error within the immediate area of a signalbox.

Track Circuits

Mention of track circuits demands the explanation of a basically simple electric circuit which is used to perform many functions in railway signalling. Track circuits are installed at many semaphore boxes and in all power-operated boxes. Each track is divided into sections, usually between each signal but also through points and crossings, and each section has its own track circuit. At each end of the track circuit, insulated fishplates are employed to prevent current

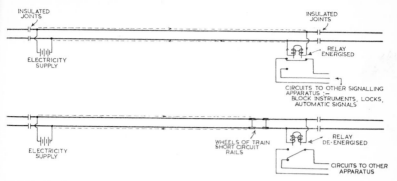

FIG 23 Simplified diagram of a track circuit shown at the top unoccupied and at the bottom occupied.

from one circuit reaching that of another. All rail joints within the one track circuit are bonded with wire to reduce the electrical resistance of the intermediate fishplated joints. Each track circuit is fed at one end with a low-voltage electric current. At the other end the track circuit is connected to a relay. Normally when a track section is unoccupied the circuit is completed and the relay is energised. When a locomotive or train occupies the track circuit it short circuits the current, through its wheels. This leaves the relay without any current and its arm therefore drops away. The movement of the relay arm is used to make or break other electrical circuits connected to associated signalling equipment. In its simplest form it can be made to operate an indicator or illuminate lights on a signalbox diagram to show the signalman that the track is occupied. It can also be used to lock signals and points and to prevent a second train from being signalled into the back of the first. In automatic colour-light areas, the action of the relay is utilised to set each signal to danger as a train passes it. When the train passes off the track circuit, the signal it controls will clear to a proceed aspect. Thus as a train proceeds, the signals behind it go to danger and, later, clear solely by track circuit occupation and clearance. Sometimes only one rail is insulated for track circuit purposes; in other cases both rails are insulated. On electrified lines special precautions are taken to ensure that track circuits cannot be affected by the traction current. For many years this was achieved by employing current opposite to that used for the traction supply, that is alternating current track circuits with direct current electric trains and vice-versa. In modern installations where high voltage ac traction supply is used, track circuits are of the ac or dc type but both must be immunised against false operation from the traction supply.

This then is the track circuit in its basic conventional form as it is used today on most British Railways and London Transport lines. The quest for higher train speeds, improved maintenance procedures and the need for track circuits to serve functions other than train detection has led signal engineers to experiment with other forms of track circuit. For many years it has been apparent that the weakest part of the track is the joint between adjacent lengths of rail, and long continuous welded rail is gradually being installed on heavily-used BR lines. As we have just seen track circuits rely on insulated joints at section ends which mean that fishplated joints must be retained at track circuit boundaries. To overcome this problem and to help eliminate rail joints experiments have been undertaken with jointless track circuits which employ high frequency coded alternating currents, transmitted at one end of the track circuit section, and received by equipment at the other end which responds only to the frequency of that particular section. Frequencies employed for this type of track circuit are carefully selected to provide adequate variation for adjacent track circuits on the same or nearby lines. So far in Britain this form of track circuit has not been fully proved for electrified lines because of the risk of interference from the traction supply, but experiments are in hand with modified versions which might well have formed the basis of signalling through the Channel Tunnel.

This modern development of the track circuit however is not only used to detect the presence of a train but can be employed to pass coded signals from the track to the train as the basis for cab signalling, described in more detail in the section on automatic train control.

Treadles

In older installations, or in localities where track circuits are unsuitable, treadles are employed. A treadle takes the form of a metal strip which is fixed against the inside face of the running rail, and at the same height as the top of the rail. It thus normally fouls the flangeway. The bar has short ramps at each end and is pivoted to enable it to be depressed by the flanges of passing trains. When depressed, an electrical contact is broken and an indication is registered in the signalbox in the same way as with track circuits. However, treadles can only give local indications owing to the practical restriction on their length; also, as they normally foul the flangeway, their use on high speed running lines, although not unknown, is undesirable. A more modern form of treadle, more accurately known as a striker, is employed in some areas. This consists of a short wire rod which is placed at an angle against the inside of the running rail, and which, when depressed by a train, operates the appropriate circuit.

Axle Counters

The treadle suffers by the fact that it does not give a continuous indication of the state of the line, for it shows only the last event to take place. When a train passes over a treadle the treadle indicates only that a train has in fact passed over it. Unless the train stops on the treadle there is no indication as to the subsequent whereabouts of the train. Where treadles are used, as a train passes over a treadle to enter a section, certain signalling equipment may be locked until the train passes a second treadle at the far end of the section. But the operation of the two treadles is no guarantee that the whole train has passed through the section. If part of the train is left in the section, when the front part operates the treadle on leaving the section it may free the equipment. A piece of equipment which overcomes this difficulty is the axle counter. This is operated by a form of treadle, and electrically records the total number of axles passing over it

Normally one counter is installed at the entrance to a section, a second one at the exit. Equipment locked to protect a train as it enters the section will not become free until the second counter has recorded an identical number of axles leaving the section. Axle counters avoid the need for continuous track circuiting, which on long sections can be expensive and complicated. Axle counters are popular on overseas railways but are used on British Railways only in a few places, where track circuits cannot be used and ordinary treadles are unsuitable.

Rule K3 (formerly Rule 55)

If a train has been stopped by a signal at danger the train crew may be required to take action to ensure that the signalman does not overlook the train. This is often achieved by the secondman or guard, whoever is nearest, going to the signalman within a stipulated time (usually two minutes, but in some cases, particularly in fog, immediately) to remind the signalman of the situation. While in the signalbox the trainman must see that the signalman uses devices such as lever collars (a metal plate slipped on to a signal or point lever handle which prevents the lever from being operated) to protect the train. This action is now known as section K3, formerly rule 55—in the past one of the most often quoted rules in the rule book. However, the train may be delayed for several minutes more after the line is clear for it to proceed while the guard or secondman walks back to the train from the signalbox. To avoid a lengthy walk from the signal to the signalbox, many stop signals are provided with a lineside telephone, or a plunger which when operated by the secondman or driver works a bell, buzzer or drop-flap in the signalbox to remind the signalman of the train. The signal post bears an indicator plate (see page 52) denoting that a plunger or telephone is provided. In this case too the telephone or plunger must be used by the train crew within a stipulated time in the event of delay. In other places the line is track circuited and the signalman knows from an illuminated diagram or a track circuit indicator in the signalbox that a train is at the signal. In such cases, and on some lines where lock-and-block signalling is used, the signal post carries a white diamond-shaped plate (see page 49) indicating to the crew that the signal is exempt from rule K3 and that they need take no action except for prolonged delay. A telephone may be provided at the signal so that the crew can speak to the signalman if necessary. Rule K3 need not be carried out on single lines if the driver is in possession of the train staff on staff and ticket lines, or an electric staff, tablet or token, or on lines operated by tokenless block. Where a shunting move is made on a running line, the shunter carries out rule K3 immediately if the movement is detained. Here, too, if the line is track circuited and rule K3 need not be carried out the fact may be denoted by a white diamond sign superimposed on the red band of a disc signal.

On track circuit block lines practically all stop signals are provided with telephones to the controlling signalbox. In certain clearly defined circumstances if the telephone at the signal is out of order and the train crew cannot communicate with the signalman from any other telephone the train may pass the signal at danger and proceed very cautiously ahead towards the next signal, ready to stop short of any obstruction.

5—The Block System

In Chapter 1 we saw how the block system became established as the standard method for the safe working of trains. Despite recent large-scale introductions of power signalling with colour-light signals and extensive track circuiting, much of British Railways is still worked on the block telegraph system, in which signalmen communicate with the men in adjacent boxes regarding train movements by block telegraph instruments and bells, and work signals and points mechanically from levers through wire or rodding.

Originally the positioning of signalboxes was largely governed by the track layout, for when the grouping of points and signal levers in a signalbox had become established, the Board of Trade decreed that mechanically-worked points should not be more than 250 (later 350) yd from the signalbox which controlled them. Thus, at a large junction station, several signalboxes were required, sometimes no more than ¼-mile apart, solely to control sets of points. But they also had to have signals and were equipped with block instruments and bells for the block system. Most country stations had signalboxes to control points connecting sidings to the main line and, generally speaking, block sections ran from station to station. In some instances, however, where stations were several miles apart, the block sections would have been inconveniently long and one or more intermediate signalboxes were provided solely to divide the line into additional block sections to permit the operation of a greater number of trains, for the overall frequency of trains on a line is governed by the time taken in passing through the longest block section. These intermediate boxes often had but four levers, controlling a distant and home signal in each direction. In recent years, by substituting power-operated points and signals, many intermediate signalboxes, and boxes provided solely for the control of one or two sets of points, have been abolished and their function transferred to an adjacent box.

Although many safety devices have been added to block instruments to prevent errors by signalmen in the operation of the block system, they have been superimposed on the working of block instruments and basically the method of communication between signal boxes has changed little since the adoption of the block system. Changes that have been made are in detail—variations in the design of block instrument casing and face, and in the method of displaying the block indications, and changes in the block bell code from time to time, particularly in recent years in an attempt to standardise the bell codes used in different regions.

As we explained earlier, the principle of the absolute block system, which is used on lines carrying passenger trains, is that there shall not be more than one train in a block section on the same line at the same time. The definition of a block section is: the section of line from the most advanced starting signal controlled by one box to the outermost home signal controlled by the next signalbox ahead. The section of line from the outermost home signal of one box to the most advanced starting signal controlled by the *same* box is termed station limits. This is under the jurisdiction of one signalman for it lies entirely between signals which he alone controls. He can make certain train movements within station limits without reference to the signalmen in the adjacent boxes. If the

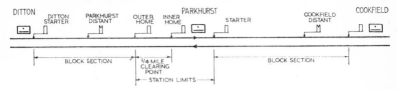

FIG 24 Diagram illustrating the limits of a block section, station limits and the clearing point.

signalling permits, there can be more than one train in station limits on the same line at one time as we shall see later.

In Chapter 2 we mentioned the clearing point in advance of the outermost home signal to which the line must be clear in addition to the block section before a signalman may accept under normal conditions a train from the signalman in the rear. On some lines, the interpretation of the block section includes this section of line beyond the home signal to the clearing point.

Three-Position Block Instruments

The basic equipment in a signalbox for the operation of the block system comprises the block telegraph instruments and single stroke bells. The block instruments have a dial resembling in some ways a clock face but instead of figures there are three panels labelled line blocked (or normal), line clear and train on line respectively. Instead of two hands there is only one, rather like a compass needle, pivoted in the centre and free to swing either to right or left. (In the latest BR block instruments the needle covers only the lower half of the dial, for the three panels themselves are also on the lower half).

The needle is normally vertical and pointing at the line blocked panel; it is deflected diagonally to point at the line clear or train on line panels by electromagnetic coils inside the instrument.

There are two types of block instrument—a pegging instrument and a non-pegging instrument. The pegging instrument has a commutator handle

FIG 25 The three indications shown by a three-position block instrument.

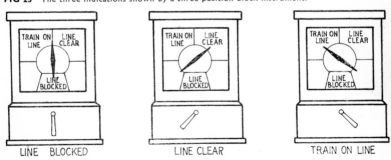

under the block instrument face, which is turned to right or left by the signalman to operate the block indicator needle. A non-pegging instrument has no pegging handle and electrically repeats the indication shown by the block instrument in another signalbox. The block instruments in one signalbox are connected electrically to those in the next box through the lineside telegraph wires or by buried cables.

The signalmen in the boxes at both ends of a block section need to know the state of the section, so that each box is equipped with a block indicator for the same line. The box in advance of the block section (the exit end) has a pegging instrument, for the signalman there, in effect, is in charge of the section since it is he who decides whether it is safe for a train to enter the block section and approach his signalbox. The signalbox in the rear of the block section (the entry end) has a repeater instrument which displays the same indications as on the corresponding pegging instrument at the box ahead. But as each signalbox is the boundary between two block sections it will have two instruments, a repeater for the advance section and a pegging instrument for the rear section. Similarly there will be two instruments for the line running in the opposite direction. Thus each box controlling double track line will have four block indicators, two of which are actually operated by the signalmen there. For each additional through line two more indicators are provided. Generally the up and down line indicators for the lines in the same block section are mounted together one above the other. Only one bell and bell tapper is provided for each pair of up and down lines in each block section, so that bell signals for both up and down trains are sent on the same bell instruments. The bell tapper or plunger operates the corresponding bell in the signalbox at the other end of the section. Fig 26 illustrates the layout of levers, block instruments and bells for a box controlling a double track line.

Method of Signalling

To follow the signalling of a train let us imagine we are in Parkhurst signalbox which is between Ditton signalbox and Cookfield signalbox. The line between Ditton and Cookfield is of double track but we are only interested in one—the down line. All signals are at danger or caution and there are no trains between Ditton and Cookfield; thus the block indicators are at line blocked, for the line is considered, in theory, to be blocked until required to be cleared for a train. A train is ready to proceed from Ditton through Parkhurst to Cookfield. The signalman at Ditton calls the attention of the signalman at Parkhurst by giving one beat on the bell, which Parkhurst acknowledges by replying with one beat. When Ditton hears the single beat in reply he knows that Parkhurst is ready and waiting. The Ditton signalman then rings the 'Is line clear?' bell signal for the type of train (let us assume an express—4 beats) to Parkhurst. If the block section is clear and the line is clear to the clearing point beyond the Parkhurst home signal, the Parkhurst signalman can accept the train from Ditton by repeating the 4-beat bell signal back to Ditton and placing the block indicator for the Ditton-Parkhurst down line block instrument at line clear. The repeater block indicator for the Ditton-Parkhurst down line at Ditton will also show line clear. The Ditton signalman can now clear his down line signals for the train. When the train leaves Ditton the signalman there sends 2 beats

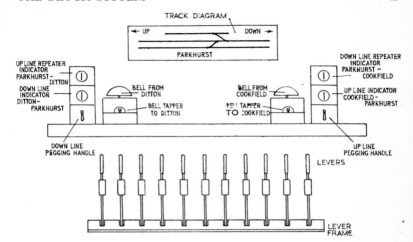

FIG 26 Typical signal box layout of block instruments, track diagram and levers.

on the bell to Parkhurst signifying train entering section and replaces his signals to danger behind the train. The Parkhurst signalman returns the 2-beat bell signal to Ditton and places the Ditton-Parkhurst down line indicator to train on line which is again repeated on the Ditton indicator. Parkhurst now offers the train to the Cookfield signalman by the same procedure. If the line is clear to Cookfield's clearing point, Cookfield will acknowledge the 4-beat bell signal and place the Parkhurst-Cookfield block indicator to line clear which will be repeated in Parkhurst box. Parkhurst can now clear his down line signals for the express. When the train passes Parkhurst, the signalman there sends the train entering section bell signal to Cookfield who acknowledges it and places the Parkhurst-Cookfield indicator at train on line.

Meanwhile, Parkhurst restores his signals to danger behind the train and having seen the tail lamp on the last vehicle of the train, which indicates that it is complete, and when the train has passed beyond the clearing point, Parkhurst calls the attention of Ditton by one beat on the bell. When Ditton acknowledges with one beat, Parkhurst sends the train out of section bell signal (2—1) to Ditton, which Ditton acknowledges by 2—1. Parkhurst also releases the block indicator from train on line to line blocked. The Ditton-Parkhurst section is now normal and Ditton may offer Parkhurst the next train if it is ready and due to go. During this time Cookfield in his turn has offered forward and had accepted the first train and cleared his signals. When the train passes Cookfield, the signalman there calls Parkhurst and gives him the 2—1 bell signal which Parkhurst acknowledges, and Cookfield releases the Parkhurst—Cookfield block indicator to line blocked. Thus Parkhurst can now offer another train to Cookfield if he has one.

In certain cases, where block sections are short, a signalman would delay a

Above left: A Tyers two-position block instrument, which survived until recently on the Southern Region.

Above right: The standard LNER type three-position pegging block instrument.

[*G. Ogilvie*

Left: Two examples of BR standard block instruments showing, on the left, an absolute block pegging instrument and on the right a permissive block instrument. The up line (top) indicator on this instrument shows only absolute block indications.

[*British Railways*

train if he waited until he received train entering section before offering the train forward. In this case the train approaching (1—2—1) signal is used. In our example when Ditton sends train entering section to Parkhurst, Parkhurst immediately sends train approaching to Cookfield who, if the line is clear, offers the train to the next box. In some places trains are signalled forward through several sections to a holding box where the signalman holds the code until he receives train entering section or train approaching.

Earlier in this chapter we explained the purpose of the clearing distance beyond the home signal which must be kept clear before a signalman can normally accept a train from the signalbox in the rear. Very often there are points or crossings in this overlap and it is, of course, necessary for these points to be correctly set for the line on which the train is to approach otherwise the overlap is valueless. If a train overshot the home signal and passed over trailing points set from another line the train might be derailed. At facing junctions where approaching trains have a choice of two or more routes it may not be possible for the signalman to set the junction points for the correct route and obtain $\frac{1}{4}$-mile clearance beyond the home signal, perhaps because a train has already been signalled across the junction in the opposite direction. In this case the signalman may set the points for another route, provided of course that the line is clear to the clearing point on this second route, in order to accept the train and prevent it from being stopped at the previous signalbox. By the time the train nears his box the junction may have become unoccupied. But the signalman may not reset the points for the correct route and clear the signals until the train has been checked or, in some instances, stopped momentarily at the home signal.

If for any reason a signalman cannot accept a train from the signalman in the rear because, for example, points within the overlap cannot be correctly set or if another train on a conflicting route has been signalled, he will intimate this refusal by not acknowledging the Is line clear? bell signal and will maintain the block indicator at line blocked. The signalman in the rear knows his colleague has refused the train since he will have obtained an acknowledgement of his call attention bell signal. If a train is refused the signalman must send the Is line clear? code at intervals of a few minutes until the signalman ahead can accept the train. If the signalman at the box ahead refuses a train the signalman offering the train must stop it at his signals. This he does by keeping all the signals for the train at danger. When the train has almost stopped at the home signal this may be cleared to let the train draw up to the starter; as the train approaches this signal it too may be cleared (except in fog) to let the train forward to the advanced starter where it is finally stopped to await acceptance. This action of checking a train at each signal applies in semaphore areas whatever the layout and the signalman must ensure that the train is under control before he lets it run towards the starting or advanced starting signal. If a train is awaiting acceptance at the advanced starter and is beyond the clearing point the signalman may accept another train from the rear. When this train arrives it too may be allowed to draw forward to the inner home so that there can thus be two trains within station limits.

As an additional reminder, the times at which all bell signals are sent and received are usually recorded by each signalman in his train register book. The times when signalmen come on and go off duty are also entered, as are any unusual occurrences, as for example, when a secondman or guard carries out Rule K3. At busy signalboxes, a booking man may be employed solely for this duty and to make and answer telephone calls regarding train movements, while the signalman concentrates on the actual signalling of trains.

Two-Position Block Indicators

The block indicators we have described are known as three-position instruments from the number of indications which they show. On a few lines, old types of two-position block instruments are still used but they are obsolete and most are to be replaced with modern equipment. The two-position block indicator usually takes the form of a miniature semaphore arm, either horizontal or lowered at 45 degrees. The disadvantage of this type of instrument is that it can show only two indications to cover the three sequences in three-position block signalling. Thus one indication must have two meanings. Usually line blocked and train on line were indicated by the arm being in the horizontal position and line clear with the arm lowered. This was by no means universal, however, and some companies used other combinations of indications. The two-position block indicator was developed in the early days of the block system as an alternative to the needle telegraph instrument. It was intended to look like a signal and, in effect, showed when the starting signal at the signal box in the rear could be cleared.

Block Locking

The block system in its basic form was not proof against human error. There was nothing to stop a signalman mistakenly giving train out of section, clearing the block indicator and giving a second line clear while the first train was still in the block section, perhaps having broken down. Nor was there anything to stop him clearing his signals for a train that had not been accepted by the signalman at the box ahead. To prevent just such occurrences, signal engineers devised various types of locking between block instruments, signals and the track, the object of which is to ensure that trains are correctly signalled on the block instruments and that trains cannot be overlooked. One of the most widely used was the Sykes Lock and Block system, which survives in one or two places on BR although it is now virtually obsolete.

Sykes Lock and Block

In the Sykes system a signalman cannot clear a starting signal to admit a train into the block section ahead until the signal has been electrically released by the signalman at the next box ahead. This man is prevented from giving such a release until (1) the previous train has passed a specified signal at that box, (2) that signal has been returned to danger behind the train, and (3) the train has operated a treadle on the track to prove that it had in fact proceeded a safe distance beyond the signal. Special block and signal indicators are used to show the state of the block section, and whether signals are locked or free. (Fig 27) The type of indicator depicted would be used at a signalbox having only a home signal which also controls admission to the block section ahead. If a signalbox has a home and a starting signal, the home signal instrument would not have a

Above: The Western Region box at East Usk is an example of a modern mechanical signal box. The short-handled levers control power points and signals. [*British Railways*

Below: Liverpool Street West Side box before the 1949 electrification and resignalling was a typical example of a large mechanical box with lever frames on both sides of the operating floor. [*British Railways*

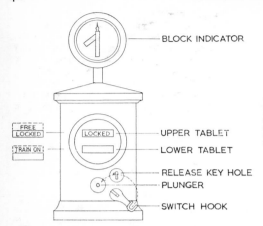

BLOCK INDICATOR

FREE
LOCKED

LOCKED — UPPER TABLET

TRAIN ON

LOWER TABLET

RELEASE KEY HOLE

PLUNGER

SWITCH HOOK

FIG 27 A Sykes block indicator used in lock and block signalling. The instrument depicted would be used at a signal box having only a home signal which also controls admission to the block section ahead.

block indicator and the starting signal instrument would not have a switch hook or lower tablet aperture. If a signalbox controls several stop signals on the same line, each intermediate signal would have a corresponding Sykes instrument with only an upper tablet aperture.

The method of offering and accepting trains is generally similar to that used with normal three-position block instruments. As an example suppose we have two signalboxes called Lee and Mottingham and that the previous train has passed Mottingham. Lee wishes to send another down train to Mottingham, so he calls attention on the bell. If Mottingham can accept the train the signalman there acknowledges the Is line clear? code and presses the plunger on his home signal instrument. This causes the lower tablet on his instrument to change from blank to train on, and the upper tablet at Lee to change from locked to free. It also unlocks Lee's starting signal and places the block indicator at Lee in the raised position. When Lee clears his starting signal the indicator's upper tablet changes to locked and the signal becomes locked until the train has passed beyond it and operated a treadle. This action changes the upper tablet to free, unlocks the signal which may then be returned to danger, but the upper tablet then again shows locked and the signal is locked at danger behind the train. Lee, of course, gives the train entering section bell signal which Mottingham acknowledges and places the switch hook over the plunger. Mottingham may then offer the train forward to the next box and, if accepted, clear his signals, which causes the upper tablet on the Mottingham instrument to show locked. When the train reaches Mottingham and passes over the treadle the signalman may restore his signals to danger behind the train. The upper tablet there shows locked again and the lower tablet blank. Mottingham removes the switch hook from the plunger, which lowers the block indicator at Lee, and gives Lee the train out of section bell signal which Lee acknowledges. The section is now normal again and Lee may offer the next train.

In some places the treadle has been replaced by track circuits to serve the same function. The Sykes system with detailed variations was used by a number of pre-grouping companies, particularly the SE & C, LSW and GE railways. On some lines the semaphore block indicator worked in reverse and was raised for line clear. The Midland used a rotary interlocking block instrument in which the block instrument operating handle could only be worked through the correct sequence and the block indicator was interlocked with the signals.

From these and other types of block instrument locking have been developed the modern block locking controls which are now standard on all main lines retaining the manual block system.

Modern Block Controls

The basis of modern block controls are two track circuits on each line at each signalbox. One is placed immediately to the rear of the outermost home signal (the berth track circuit), the other generally in the rear of the starting signal but usually beyond the clearing point. The signal controlling entry to the block section can only be cleared (usually for one pull only) when the block indicator for the section ahead is at line clear. This indicator can only be pegged at line clear when the berth track circuit at the box ahead is clear and its home and distant signal arms are respectively at danger and caution. This latter control is known as interlinking. In our earlier example of three boxes—Ditton, Parkhurst and Cookfield—the signalman at Parkhurst can only peg up line clear on the Ditton-Parkhurst instrument when his home and distant signals are at danger and caution respectively and the home signal berth track circuit is clear. The Ditton signalman can only clear his starting signal towards Parkhurst when the Ditton-Parkhurst block indicator is at line clear. When the train approaches Parkhurst it occupies the berth track circuit at the home signal. This action will place the Ditton-Parkhurst block indicator at train on line if Parkhurst has for any reason not already pegged it in that position. If the train cannot proceed immediately and has to be held at the home signal its occupation of the berth track circuit will maintain the block indicator at train on line even if Parkhurst inadvertently forgets the train and unpegs the operating handle to normal.

The second track circuit, to the rear of the starting signal, may also control the block indicator for the rear section (in the case of Parkhurst, the Ditton-Parkhurst indicator). Once the rear section block indicator has been placed at line clear, it cannot be placed at line clear for a second time until one or both of the

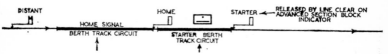

When occupied places or maintains the rear section block indicator at train on line.

When line clear has been pegged on rear section block indicator both track circuits must usually be occupied and cleared before line clear can be pegged for a second time. The starter must be at danger before the home signal can be cleared.

FIG 28 Track circuits used in conjunction with modern block controls.

E

track circuits have been occupied and cleared, thus proving that a train has passed through the rear section. This feature is often referred to as Welwyn control following its introduction after a collision at Welwyn Garden City in 1935. The signalman cannot forget to work his signals and just leave them at clear since he cannot place the rear section block indicator at line clear if he did. And he cannot restore only the home signal to danger to peg up line clear since the sequential locking ensures that the signals must be returned to danger behind a train before they can be cleared a second time. These features—the two track circuits, interlinking, line clear release and sequential locking—ensure that trains are correctly signalled and prove that once signalled, a train must pass through the section before a second train can be signalled.

Cancellation

To cover the possibility of a train not proceeding after being signalled, the signalmen have means of overcoming the locks on the block controls in such circumstances. In the case of Sykes instruments a special release key is used by the signalman to unlock the instrument; rotary block instruments have a release plunger to cancel a line clear indication, which must be operated by the signalmen at both ends of the section simultaneously; other boxes have special release plungers which are sometimes sealed or which may have a time delay incorporated to prevent the immediate clearance of a conflicting route.

Signalboxes Close Together

Where signalboxes are no more than ½- to ¾-mile apart, the distant signal for one box may be under the starting and/or home signal of the signal box to the rear as we have seen in the chapter on signals. If the boxes are even closer together, then the distant signal for the rear box may also act as the outer distant for the next box. Thus the signalmen at both boxes must exercise control over the operation of the outer distant. This can be done mechanically by slotting as described in chapter 4 but this is unusual in the case of distant signals.

At some locations the forward box has no direct control of the outer distant and in this instance the rear signalman must be given an indication as to when he may clear the distant signal. On the Western Region this is sometimes done by the use of a special bell signal. Suppose we have three signalboxes—Northolt East, Northolt West and Ruislip—the first two being, say, 500yd apart. If Northolt East offers a train to Northolt West, before accepting the train West box must first offer it to Ruislip. If Ruislip accepts it then Northolt West can accept it from Northolt East in the normal way and the East box signalman can clear all his signals. If Ruislip refuses the train or if the previous train is still in the section between Northolt West and Ruislip, then the Northolt West signalman will return the bell signal 2—2—2 to Northolt East, which the latter must acknowledge before the West box signalman pegs up line clear. Northolt East in this case must not clear his signals until the train has passed the distant signal which is of course at caution.

Elsewhere what is known as indicator working is in force. When the signalman at the forward box clears his distant signal lever an indicator in the rear box changes from caution to clear and only then may the rear box signalman

FIG 29 The warning arrangement.

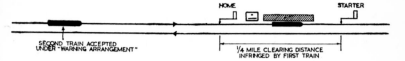

clear his distant signal. At many places however the outer distant, though perhaps a semaphore signal, is electrically controlled by both boxes and it will only clear when the distant levers in both are reversed.

The Warning Arrangement—Regulation 5

Earlier in this chapter we explained that it is necessary under normal working for the line to be clear to the clearing point before a signalman can accept a train. In certain circumstances, however, trains may be accepted with the line clear to the outermost home signal only and with no clearance beyond. Thus there is no margin of error if a driver misjudges the braking distance and if he overruns the signal he may collide with another train. For that reason this working is restricted in use and, where it is permitted, cannot usually be applied if passenger trains are involved. It is however regularly used if a signalman accepts a freight train stopping to shunt at a siding in the block section or an officer's special train stopping in the section to make an inspection of the line, for it may be inconvenient to keep the ¼-mile clearing distance free for say ½-hour or more with a normal acceptance. Elsewhere, it may be used only where authorised by the operating department or, in some cases, during emergency working, as provided for in the signalling regulations.

Because there is no over-run beyond the home signal the driver of a train accepted under this regulation must be warned at the previous signalbox. For this reason it is often known as the warning arrangement. In this example we will call the two signalboxes concerned Paxton and Ganwick. Paxton offers Ganwick a freight train stopping in section (bell signal 2—2—3). If the line is clear to Ganwick's home signal he accepts the train by sending Paxton the bell signal 3—5—5. If Paxton is ready to send the train he will acknowledge this signal by returning bell signal 3—5—5 after which Ganwick will place the block indicator at line clear. The Paxton signalman must now warn the driver of the train that it has been accepted under Regulation 5. This he does by leaving his signals at danger to check the train's speed. The signalman then clears the home signal when the train has nearly stopped and as the train approaches the signalbox the signalman displays a steady green hand signal (flag by day, lamp by night) to the driver who must acknowledge the hand signal by a short blast on the locomotive horn. The signalman may then clear the starting signal(s). The driver understands by the hand signal that the train has been accepted under the warning arrangement and not that he should pass the signal at danger, for generally a driver must never pass a danger signal unless he receives verbal instructions to do so. In certain cases where the warning arrangement is regularly used, a fixed warning signal (see chapter 2) is used underneath the most advanced starting signal, but the warning signal may only be cleared when the train has nearly stopped at it. If a train not stopping in the block section has been accepted in this way and the clearing distance then becomes free before it enters the section the signalman at the box ahead may send the 3—3—5 bell signal to the rear signal box to indicate that the line is clear including the clearing distance and that the train need not be stopped and warned.

Other Regulations

So far, we have described the working of the block system for normal moves, but the signalling regulations cover all eventualities found in railway working, including the signalling of certain shunting moves, a train assisted by an engine in the rear, working through the block section in the wrong direction and for various types of emergency. Some of the special moves, such as working in the wrong direction, may only be used where authorised, while emergency working is described in a later chapter. We said at the start of this chapter that a signalman can make certain train movements within station limits without reference to the signalmen at the boxes on each side of him. However he cannot signal a move which will infringe the clearing distance inside the home signal without first obtaining permission from the signalman in the rear box. This he does by sending the blocking back inside home signal bell signal (2—4) to the box in the rear and, when acknowledged, he must place the block indicator at train on line. After the shunting move has been made and the clearing distance becomes free the signalman sends the obstruction removed (2—1) bell signal to the rear in the same manner as train out of section. This regulation is used at any time when the clearing point is infringed such as at a facing junction when the junction points are reversed towards a line on which a train is standing within the clearing distance on that line. It is also possible to shunt outside the home signal into the block section. In this case the blocking back outside home signal bell code (3—3) must first be sent to the box in the rear and acknowledged. Of course neither of these moves may be made if a train has already been accepted from the box in the rear.

Some lines close at night in which case the signalboxes close after the last train has run. This the signalmen do by exchanging the bell signal 7—5—5. They open the following morning by exchanging the bell signal 5—5—5 followed by a test of the block instruments and bells (16 beats).

On lines with a 24-hour service it is often possible and economical to close, perhaps for the night shift, certain signalboxes which do not control junctions or other points which must be reset during this period. The block section is of course then lengthened. For example in the case of Ditton, Parkhurst and Cookfield, if Parkhurst closes, the block section is from Ditton's most advanced starting signal to Cookfield's outermost home signal. If a box has no block controls the signalman at the box to be closed sends the 7—5—5 bell signal in each direction and, after receiving acknowledgement, turns the block closing switch which connects the forward section block instrument and bell circuits to those of the rear section (cutting out the instruments in the box which is closing) and finally clears the signals in both directions. If the box has full block locking controls it is a little more complicated, for the signalman at Parkhurst must obtain a line clear from the box ahead in each direction for a minute or so in order to clear his signals. In this case he uses the 5—5—7 bell signal instead. A box can only switch out when the block indicators are at line blocked. After the middle box has switched out the signalmen at the boxes on each side must then test the block bells and indicators to ensure that communication has correctly been established between them.

When opening a signalbox the signalman must first telephone the signalmen at the boxes on each side to enquire if any trains are signalled, for he must not switch in his block instruments if the indicators are at line clear. When he can switch in, he turns the block switch, sends the 5—5—5 bell signal to the adjacent boxes and, if a train is not approaching, restores the signals to danger. Provided no trains have been signalled he must then test the block instruments and bells.

Intermediate Block Signals

In the opening of this chapter we described how the siting of signalboxes became established and how intermediate signalboxes were necessary to provide additional, shorter block sections. Many of these boxes controlled nothing more than home and distant signals for each line. For many years it has been the practice to abolish these intermediate signalboxes where possible, but to avoid lengthening the block section the signals have been retained, although control of them has been transferred to another signalbox, usually the signalbox to the rear. More recently, two-aspect colour-light intermediate block home and distant signals have been used instead of semaphores, for intermediate block signals, as they are called (abbreviated to IBS), are usually electrically controlled. In some respects the arrangement is like an extra advanced starting signal but provided with its own distant signal.

Figure 30 illustrates a typical IBS arrangement in which we have our examples Ditton, Parkhurst and Cookfield, but in this case Parkhurst signalbox has been abolished and replaced with intermediate block signals.

It is possible to have two trains on each line between Ditton and Cookfield, separated by the IB home signal. The down line is continuously track circuited from Ditton's most advanced starting signal up to and for an overlap (similar to the ¼-mile clearing point) beyond the down IB home signal so that the Ditton signalman knows when a train has passed out of the intermediate block section into the block section proper.

The block section controlled by block instruments runs from signal D5 to C2 on the down line and from signal C25 to D22 on the up. The signalling is quite straightforward. We shall assume that there are no trains between Ditton and

FIG 30 Intermediate block signals.

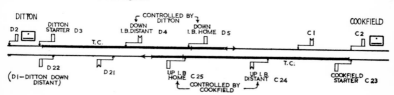

Cookfield. A down train is accepted by Ditton from the previous box. When Ditton receives the train entering section signal from the rear box the Ditton signalman may clear signals D2, D3 and D1 which gives the train a clear run as far as the IB home (signal D5). Ditton may then offer the train to Cookfield and, if accepted, Ditton clears the IB signals D5 and D4. As the train passes Ditton, the signalman there sends train entering section to Cookfield. As the train passes beyond the IB distant and home signals they return automatically to caution and danger respectively and cannot clear a second time until the Ditton signalman restores the lever to danger and clears it again ('lever' because usually both IB home and distant signals are worked from one lever). In some cases the IB signals do not return automatically to danger or caution.

As soon as the first train has passed clear of the overlap track circuit beyond the IB home signal D5, Ditton may clear his signals D2, D3 and D1 for a second train to proceed towards the IB home. When the first train passes Cookfield, the signalman there gives train out of section and Ditton may now offer the second train and, if accepted, clear the IB signals. In this case the Ditton signalman gives the train entering section signal only when the second train is accepted and not as it passes the box if the first train is still in the block section. A buzzer sounds momentarily in the signalbox controlling the IB signals when a train passes the IB home signal to advise the signalman that the train has entered the section.

The Permissive Block System

Having spent much of this book in emphasising the object of the absolute block system—that there shall not be more than one train in a block section on one line at one time—we come now to the system where it *is* possible to have more than one train in a block section on one line at one time—called Permissive Block. It may be used only where specially authorised and is confined to use on goods lines, or to goods trains when running on passenger lines or, more rarely, for passenger trains at certain stations where the platform lines are within a block section and it is necessary for two or more trains to be at the same platform together. Permissive block is often used on goods lines at the approaches to a yard and allows several freight trains to bunch together instead of being spread over several block sections as would be necessary under absolute block regulations.

The signalboxes where permissive working is authorised are usually equipped with special block instruments, similar to those for absolute block but having, in addition, an indicator which must be set by the signalman to show how many trains are in the section. This is not usually electrically repeated on the corresponding instrument in the rear signalbox and the signalman there must work his own counter indicator.

There need be no clear overlap beyond the home signal in order to accept trains under permissive working. With this exception, the method of signalling a single train is similar to absolute block. The essential difference lies in the fact that the signalman in the rear can offer a second train while the first train is still in the section and while the block indicator is at train on line. The signalman in the rear sends the Is line clear? code for the class of train but the signalman at the box ahead will accept it by the bell signal line occupied acceptance (2—4—2) and leave the block indicator at train on line. When the second train enters the section the train entering section bell signal is forwarded and acknowledged and the block indicator counters at both boxes moved to 2. Several trains can be admitted to the section in this way and for each the signalman must advance the counter accordingly. When a train leaves the section the signalman sends the train out of section bell signal to the rear and both signalmen move their counter indicators back by one. The block indicator remains at train on line until the last train has cleared the section. Where specially authorised, if no trains are in the section the next train can be accepted by the bell signal 4—3 denoting line clear to home signal. When a train is being admitted to a clear permissive block section the signals may be worked in the normal way. If a train is to be admitted to an occupied section it must be nearly stopped at the signal controlling entry to the section and then the calling-on or warning signal cleared, if provided, or, if not, the main signal. The latter indication however has a number of meanings and can be ambiguous, and calling-on signals are likely to be provided at all places where permissive working is in regular use.

It is of course essential when a passenger train is to run over a goods line or passenger line used occasionally for permissive working, that absolute working is applied both in front of and behind the passenger train, including the $\frac{1}{4}$-mile overlap beyond the home signal for acceptance, except where permissive working is specially authorised for passenger trains at certain stations. Where passenger lines are worked under permissive block regulations at these stations, and warning signals are not provided, the train is checked at the section signal which is then cleared, and a green hand signal displayed to the driver by the signalman.

Single Lines—Staff or Token Working

Single lines are worked on similar principles to those of double lines but the protection of the absolute block system is supplemented by additional safety devices, to avoid the possibility of head-on collision. Usually, but not always, the driver of a train passing over a single line section is given a visible token of authority to be on the single line. The actual form of this authority has various styles but the principles are similar—only one authority is available for one single line section at one time. It is the way in which this is achieved that varies. The three basic types of single line authority are: 1—wooden staff; 2—staff and ticket; 3—electric staff, tablet or key token. The simplest method of single line operation is by wooden staff. This method is usually confined to dead-end branches carrying only light traffic, for, by the very nature of the system with only one staff for the section, trains can only run in alternate directions—the first from A to B the second from B to A, the third from A to B and so on. There cannot be two successive trains from A to B without an intervening return working from B to A unless someone takes the staff from one end to the other which would not be very practicable. This method of working is known as one engine in steam and the staff is often referred to as an OES staff. Usually, normal block working is dispensed with because there can only be one train on the line anyway. Trains work solely by the timetable and under the authority of the wooden staff. If there are any points to be worked at the terminus end of the branch they are usually operated from a ground frame which is unlocked by a key mounted on the train staff, but the few branches of this type retaining passenger services are usually operated by diesel multiple-unit trains which do not need any shunting at the terminus.

A development of the single staff system, known as staff and ticket, is sometimes used on through-running lines where several trains may pass in one direction before one in the opposite direction. There is still only one wooden staff for the section but it is supplemented by paper tickets which are, in fact, printed forms, which the signalman must complete with details of the train concerned. The ticket is given to a driver instead of the staff and authorises him, after seeing the train staff for the section, to proceed on to the single line. The tickets are kept at each of the signalboxes concerned in locked ticket boxes which are opened and closed by a key on the staff. Thus a signalman can only open the ticket box to obtain a ticket when he has the staff. Where several trains are to follow each other in the same direction all except the last are given a ticket (and the drivers shown the train staff). The last train of a group takes the staff so that the signalman at the other end on receiving the staff can send trains through the section in the opposite direction. If a train is double-headed by two locomotives, both drivers must be given tickets if a following train is to take the staff; if not, the leading driver is given a ticket and the rear driver the staff.

Normal block instruments and bells are used in conjunction with the staff and ticket system. Separate up and down line indicators are provided as in the case of double line working even though in single line operation they apply to the same track. A signalman may not offer a train forward unless he has the train staff for the section in his possession. The staff and ticket system is simple but delays can be caused by a signalman completing a ticket and considerable

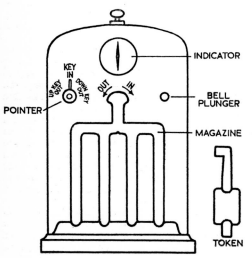

FIG 31 Single line electric key-token instrument. Later types have a block indicator instead of a pointer to show whether the line is normal or whether a token has been removed for either an up or down train.

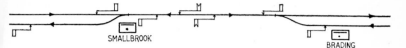

FIG 32   Track layout of the single-line section described in the text.

inconvenience may be caused when trains are late and the staff is at the wrong end of the section. The system is, however, virtually obsolete.

The various types of electric token systems which are used on the majority of BR single lines do not suffer from this defect. The two signalboxes at each end of a single line section, which are usually referred to as staff or token stations, are both equipped with a token instrument, each containing several staffs or tokens. The two instruments are electrically interlocked so that, in normal working, if a token has been taken out of either instrument it is impossible to obtain a second token until the first has been replaced in one or other instruments. There are several types of electric token instrument, different in appearance but similar in function. The three commonest are: large electric staff—a steel version of the wooden staff but with metal rings fixed along its length to ensure that it can only be placed in the instrument for which it was intended; key token—a small metal token with a key at one end, the key matching the lock release mechanism in the token instruments concerned; and the tablet—a small round flat metal disc with a hole in the centre. Every staff, token or tablet is engraved with the names of the signalboxes between which it applies. Although staffs, tokens or tablets are unique to one single line section, different lock configurations are provided for adjacent single line sections to prevent the wrong token being inserted. As the token instruments are electrically interlocked between boxes they serve as block instruments. Fig 31 shows the principal features of a key token instrument. They are: the token magazine; the bell plunger; the indicator pointer—a modified block indicator—and the needle indicator. The instruments are identical at both ends of the section. The needle indicator is deflected only by the sending of bell signals on the plunger while the indicator pointer has three positions, normal, train coming from, train going to. In this example we will call the two signalboxes Brading and Smallbrook. If Brading wishes to send a train to Smallbrook, the Brading signalman, after calling attention on the bell and receiving an acknowledgement sends the Is line clear ? bell code which Smallbrook will acknowledge if he can accept the train. The Smallbrook signalman will keep the bell plunger pressed in on giving the last beat of the bell signal and the needle indicator remains deflected. This action frees the Brading instrument and the signalman there who will already have lifted a token from the magazine into the lock can turn the token in the lock and draw it out. This causes the needle indicator at Smallbrook to be restored to the vertical position and the signalman there releases the plunger. Brading gives one beat on the bell to denote that he has obtained a token. The pointer at Brading shows train going to and that at Smallbrook train coming from. Brading may now clear the signals for the train and the train entering section bell signal is sent and acknowledged when the train enters the single line section. When the train arrives at Smallbrook the signalman there puts the token into the instrument and passes it through the lock. Smallbrook sends the train out of section bell signal which Brading acknowledges and both indicator pointers revert to normal. The instruments are now normal and may be used for signalling another train in either direction.

As the key token or tablet is rather small it is placed in a leather pouch which is attached to a metal hoop partly so that it cannot easily be mislaid, and also to make it easier for the tokens to be exchanged between a signalman and driver or secondman on a moving train. Although trains are supposed to slow down to 10 mph for a hand exchange of staffs or tokens or even stop altogether, it needs considerable skill on the part of both men, even at low speed, to hold the staff or token hoops in just the right place to ensure a perfect exchange when picking-up and setting-down tokens at the same moment, particularly by the secondman who with both hands occupied must keep his balance on a moving locomotive. Some signalboxes have lineside token holders and catchers at cab level so that the secondman can set-down and pick-up tokens as separate operations. On a number of single track main lines carrying express trains, automatic token exchange apparatus was provided at one time which, since it operated on trains passing at up to about 60 mph, avoided the need for trains to reduce speed. The apparatus was mounted on the lineside at all token exchange points and on the side of locomotives.

As in double-line signalling a signalman controlling single line sections must ensure that there is a clear overlap to the clearing point beyond the home signal before accepting a train from the box in the rear. Sometimes of necessity the clearing point is modified from the normal ¼-mile. At a passing station having two lines, both must be clear as far as the respective starting signals for a signalman to accept trains in each direction at the same time. When this occurs the signalman must keep all his signals for the two trains at danger. The first train to arrive must be stopped at the home signal, which may then be cleared to allow the train to proceed into the platform. When the signalman is sure that it has stopped inside the loop he may clear the signals for the opposing train.

Sometimes it is necessary for a shunting move to be made into the single line section outside the home signal, perhaps to clear the loop points. Where electric token instruments are in use at some places this may be done (provided no train has been accepted from the rear signalbox) without a token being given to the driver but the signalman must first have sent the blocking back bell signal and received an acknowledgement. It is also possible, where conditions permit, for blocking back shunting moves to be made at *both* ends of the section at the same time. If a train is proceeding on the single line away from a station, a shunting move may be made into the single line section behind it without the signalman sending the blocking back bell signal. However as soon as he receives train out of section for the train he must immediately forward the blocking back signal and receive an acknowledgement. Where staff and ticket working is used shunting moves are not permitted unless the blocking back signal has been exchanged and the indicator placed at train on line.

Although staff or electric token systems are still used on many British single lines, the token system is cumbersome and its operation can cause delay to trains. In some cases it can take two to three minutes for the signalman to

Above right: Automatic tablet exchange equipment seen here as the catcher on the tender snatches the pouch containing the tablet from the lineside apparatus.

Below: The driver of an SR electric multiple-unit surrenders the single line staff to the signalman at Mitcham.

[*David Chipchase*

Above left: A single-line electric token instrument.

collect the token from a train leaving the single line, operate the token instruments and signals, and hand the token to the driver of the next train entering the single line. Moreover, many diesel or electric trains have no secondman in the cab. Thus other forms of single line control have been devised which dispense with staff or token. One of the earliest was an interlocking block instrument which was linked to the signals at each end of the single line section. In more recent years direction levers have been used; as their name implies they are special levers in the signalboxes at each end of a single line section which must be set for the same direction of running and release only the signals applying to that direction. Continuous track circuiting may replace block instruments.

Single Line—Tokenless Block

Since 1967 BR has introduced tokenless block on a number of single lines, particularly on the Isle of Wight, in Scotland, and between Salisbury and Exeter. Although the block instruments differ in detail each system has similar features, particularly the short track circuit at both ends of the single line section, supplemented by a treadle at the exit end. The Scottish Region instruments are very similar in appearance and operation to existing token instruments but without the token. Starting signals are released by the block instruments on acceptance of a train for one train only. The block instruments consist of a cabinet containing the relay equipment and have a normal/reverse acceptance switch, a plunger for sending bell signals and a block indicator showing normal, train coming from and train going to indications. There is also an open cancel key and a sealed cancel plunger. To illustrate the method of working we will call the two signalboxes Usan and Montrose. For a train running from Usan to Montrose, Usan will call attention with one beat on the bell which Montrose acknowledges. Usan then sends the appropriate Is line clear ? bell signal, which if all is well Montrose acknowledges and turns his acceptance switch to reverse. Usan then holds in his ringing plunger for 5 seconds which causes the block indicator at Montrose to move to the train coming from position. Montrose replies with a 5 second plunge which places Usan's indicator at train going to and releases the lock on Usan's starting signal, which the Usan signalman can now clear. As the train enters the single line section Usan sends train entering section on the bell which is acknowledged by repetition but without further movement of the block indicator. Once the train has entered the section and occupied the entry track circuit it cannot normally be cleared from the block indicator until it has arrived at the next signalbox, occupied and cleared the overlap track circuit of the home signal and operated the treadle with the home signal clear. Having seen the train arrive complete with tail lamp the Montrose signalman calls the attention of Usan with one beat on the bell and after acknowledgement places his acceptance switch to normal which restores his own indicator to normal and gives the train out of section bell signal holding the plunger in for 5 seconds on the last beat to clear the indicator at Usan to normal. Usan acknowledges the bell signal and the equipment is then ready to pass a train in either direction. The open cancelling facility is used if the train has not entered the section and is not able to proceed and the sealed cancelling plunger is used by both signalmen concerned if a train has entered the section but cannot carry on and has to be drawn back to the end of the single line from which it started. Where signalboxes are switched out, the switching slides used to link the block instrument circuits on each side of the closed box also release the interlocking so that the signals in both directions for the main through line can be cleared together.

The tokenless block system used on the Western Region, particularly on the Salisbury-Exeter line is unusual in that it is operated on the clear block principle and there is no offering and acceptance of trains, indeed there is no bell communication, only a box-to-box telephone and the block instruments. The block instruments are of BR standard pattern adapted for single line controls with the block indications labelled normal, train accepted and train in section. There is an offer plunger, a train arrived plunger, and a normal/accept switch. In normal working signalmen must expect trains to run in timetable order. In order to illustrate the working we will call the two signalboxes Chard and Honiton. If a train is scheduled to run from Chard to Honiton and no other train is in the section and the instruments are normal, the signalman at Honiton will place his acceptance switch in the accept position. The switch at Chard must be in the normal position. When the train is ready to leave Chard or is approaching in the previous section the Chard signalman will press his offer button and provided that the acceptance switch at Honiton is in the accept position and other conditions are fulfilled the block indicators in both boxes will move to train accepted. Chard can then clear his signals for the train. As the train enters the section and occupies the entry track circuits the block indicators in both boxes automatically move to train in section. When the train has arrived at Honiton and has occupied and cleared the track circuits beyond the home signal and operated the treadle a train arrived condition is stored in the block equipment; it is confirmed after the signalman has seen the tail lamp or been advised that the train is complete by placing his acceptance switch to the normal position and operating the train arrived button, which action restores the block indicators at both boxes to normal. The section is then free for the passage of another train as soon as either of the signalmen place their acceptance switches to the accept position. A feature of the WR system is the use of ground frames unlocked by Annetts key released by track circuits at the site to allow access to intermediate sidings. Freight trains can thus shunt while occupying the main line or can be locked inside clear of the main line to allow other trains to pass. Train arrived and offer plungers at the ground frame operated in conjunction with the Annetts key, the track circuits through the siding points, which can detect which way a train is travelling, and the normal block circuits, allow train crews to clear the block instruments for the whole section to normal after a train is locked inside the sidings; they can also take up an acceptance given by both signalmen when the section is clear for the train to leave the siding. As the train enters the main line, track circuit occupation places the block indicators at train in section, and the train can proceed in either direction.

All signals on the Salisbury-Exeter line passing places were converted to colour-lights in conjunction with the tokenless block installation, with two-aspect yellow/green distants, three-aspect red/yellow/green home signals and two-aspect red/green starting signals. Full braking distance is not provided between home and starting signals and a train which must be stopped at the starting signal must first be checked at the home signal which clears to a delayed yellow as the train approaches. At passing places the main line is signalled for reversible working to allow through running when the signalbox is switched out. Since the clearance of a starting signal governing moves into the single line section is controlled by the acceptance switch at the box ahead being in the accept position, a built-in emergency feature is provided in the event of danger. In our example if Honiton becomes aware of danger before the approaching train has passed or left Chard the Honiton signalman can restore Chard's starting signal to danger by returning his acceptance switch to normal. The clear block method of working was adopted on this line as an experiment. It was designed to allow signalmen to undertake other duties away from the signalling controls but this practice has not in fact been adopted on this line. Although other WR secondary main lines have been singled subsequently, for example the Oxford-Worcester line, key token working has been employed rather than tokenless block.

On the Southern Region Isle of Wight system the block instruments are virtually normal three-position double line instruments adapted for single line use and trains are offered and accepted in the normal way.

Level Crossings

Where public roads make a level crossing of the railway they must usually be provided with gates to stop road traffic from passing over the crossing when a train is due. Until recently the gates had to close alternately across the road and the railway, but since 1958, lifting barriers which close across the road only have been permitted, (see page 89). Often level crossing gates are controlled by a signalbox which is a block post so that the signalman himself works the gates as necessary. A level crossing within the clearing point does not constitute an obstruction for the purpose of accepting a train from the rear signalbox. But the gates must be closed across the road before the signals are cleared for the train and road traffic may be held up for several minutes to allow the gates to be closed sufficiently early to give the train a clear distant signal.

Elsewhere the operation and control of level crossings varies according to the type and density of traffic on road and rail. Important crossings are worked from gate boxes manned by a crossing keeper. He must be informed of the approach of trains so that he knows when it is safe to open the gates to road traffic. This may be achieved in several ways: by providing repeater block indicators and/or bells; by telephone; by a bell or buzzer worked automatically when an approaching train operates a treadle or track circuit, or by the signalman in the adjacent block post operating a switch to release an electric lock on the

FIG 33 Level crossing worked from a ground frame.

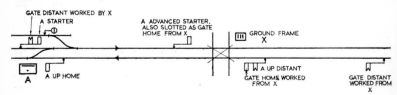

level crossing locking levers in the gate box. Sometimes gate home and distant (or distant only) signals worked by the crossing keeper protect the crossing. They look and work like ordinary signals but when used in this situation are independent of the block signals. In certain locations they may be slotted from the adjacent block post as well, to act both as block and gate signals.

On some little-used branch lines the crossing gates may normally be set across the line and opened and closed specially for a train by the secondman or guard. This is a slow process, for the train must stop, pass over the crossing and stop again. On light railways, level crossings need not have gates, but trains must reduce speed to 5 mph and whistle when approaching the road.

Crossings with private roads or farm tracks, known as occupation crossings, usually have farm-type gates set back from the railway and are normally worked by the car or lorry driver or by the farmer. There is no signalling protection and the user must stop, look and listen, before crossing. If a farmer wishes to take a herd of animals, or heavy farm machinery across the line he must first notify the local area manager who will arrange for handsignalmen to protect the crossing.

Ground Frames

At the beginning of this chapter we referred to a limit of 350yd for the mechanical operation of points, which has resulted in the provision of signalboxes with full signalling equipment solely to control, say, junction points more than 350yd from the main box. Similar situations exist on many lines where the points in question lead perhaps to sidings or a goods yard and which may be used only once or twice each day or even less. In such cases the provision of a fully-equipped signalbox may be unjustified and such points are worked from what is known as a ground frame. This is a lever-frame, often out in the open, at the site of the points, which is worked by a shunter, secondman or guard according to its purpose. There is always a locking lever and as many other levers as there are points (and sometimes shunting signals) which it controls. The locking lever, when normal, locks all the other levers normal. The locking lever is itself locked and released either electrically from a lever in the governing signalbox or by a release key. Ground frames may be used to control trailing points connecting the main line to sidings in the middle of a block section, remote from a station or signalbox or at a station which is not a block post. Telephone communication is nearly always provided between the ground frame and the signalbox to the rear. Sometimes if the siding layout permits, a local freight train may shunt back inside the yard, completely clear of the main line, after which the ground frame levers may be returned to normal and locked so that the train is locked inside. The shunter or guard then telephones to the signalman in the rear to advise him of the position and the signalman then

FIG 34 An intermediate siding controlled from a ground frame.

Left: An example of a
wooden-built mechanical
signal box. This particular
box was built by British
Railways from material
recovered from an older
LNWR box.

cancels the train on the block instruments to the box in advance. Other trains may now be signalled on the main line while the first is shunting in the yard. When shunting is complete the guard or shunter again telephones the signalman to ask for the ground frame to be released. If the situation permits, the signalman again offers the train forward to the next box and, if accepted, releases the ground frame. The last action when the train is on the main line is to relock the ground frame once more. Normally ground frames do not directly lock the signals governing entry to the block section but the release switch or lever in the signalbox will do so.

On single lines, a key on the staff or token may unlock an intermediate ground frame and, if it is permissible for the train to be locked inside, an intermediate token instrument is provided to take the token while the train is shunting so that another token can be obtained for a through train from one or other token instruments at each end of the section. When shunting is complete the guard or shunter must telephone the signalman and if the line is clear both signalmen must keep their bell plungers depressed to allow the guard or shunter to remove the token from the intermediate token instrument to unlock the ground frame. When the train is on the main line the ground frame is relocked with the token which is then taken forward on the train in the normal way.

6—Power Operation

As we have mentioned in previous chapters, power operation of points and signals is not new, but complete power installations are expensive and are only justified where savings can be made by improved traffic operation and reduced operating costs. Extensive resignalling with modern equipment is often an adjunct of electrification, for faster and more frequent trains cannot always be handled satisfactorily in areas controlled by mechanical signalling and the block telegraph system. But power control of signals and points has also been adopted in mechanical areas to improve traffic working and permit the reduction in the number of signalboxes.

Where frequent running movements were made over points more than 350yd from the main signalbox, and which were therefore unsuited to ground frame control, a second fully equipped signalbox originally had to be provided solely to work the points and associated signals. In recent years the trend has been to convert the points concerned at small installations to power operation and transfer control to the main box, thus permitting the abolition of the second signalbox. In many places, goods loops, perhaps $\frac{1}{2}$-mile long, diverge from the main line at one signalbox and rejoin the main line at the next box. Both signalboxes were needed in the past—one to control the entry points, the other the exit points. By converting one set of points to power operation one signalbox can control the whole loop. Although with the abolition of one signalbox a block section has been lost, it was only a short one and for the main line at any rate was of little value. The signals, too, come under the control of one box, although they usually remain as mechanically-worked semaphores in such cases. Where a mains electricity supply is not available to provide power, such isolated installations were sometimes worked through a hand generator set operated by the signalman, or from batteries. During the last war, a number of single-ended refuge sidings were converted to through-running loops under the control of one signal cabin by this means.

Where power-operated signals and points are worked from a mechanical lever frame the handles of the levers concerned are shortened so that the signalman can distinguish them from levers directly connected by wire or rodding. A signalman could easily injure himself if he put all the strength normally required for the pulling of a mechanically-connected lever only to find that there was no weight on it.

Pioneer Installations

The adoption of power operation provides the greatest benefit to the working of large terminal or intermediate stations and their approaches, and on lines carrying intensive traffic. In the early installations of the 1920s and 1930s one central power signalbox might take over the function of several mechanical signalboxes dispersed around a station area and approaches, and automatic signals controlled traffic on sections of plain line. But because of the cost, large and complicated centralised signal cabins were often thought not worthwhile in some power signalling schemes, and several existing mechanical signalboxes were retained. Although colour-light signals were installed, they were

F

often controlled by mechanical-type levers, while points within the 350yd limit remained mechanically operated, and others beyond this limit were converted to power operation. In some instances, too, where lines between adjacent signalboxes were not fully track circuited, block working was retained. Where lines *are* fully track circuited some of these electro-mechanical boxes, as they are called, which do not control points in frequent use may be closed at certain times and the signals they control left to function automatically, worked by the trains themselves. This is usually achieved by the reversal of the appropriate signal levers plus a king lever.

The earliest power signalling installations worked in conjunction with semaphore signals. As in mechanical signalling practice, each signal, point and facing point lock was worked from an individual lever with mechanical interlocking between levers. The levers were much smaller than the normal mechanical levers but otherwise the only difference from ordinary mechanical signalling was in the method of transmitting movement between lever and signal or points. One of the first installations of this type at Crewe was introduced in 1898 at Gresty Lane No 1 box, and was followed soon after by other boxes controlling the Crewe station area. The signals were operated by solenoids and points by electric motors.

Later, in 1918, the South Eastern & Chatham installed power signalling at Victoria in which three-position upper-quadrant semaphore signals were used. It was the first and only major scheme to have three-position semaphores, for, as we mentioned in our historical survey in Chapter 1, three- and four-aspect colour-light signals were adopted six years later and rendered three-position semaphores obsolete although those at Victoria survived until 1938.

It was the Southern Railway which led the way in the 1920s with the general introduction of power signalling at principal stations. Control of individual signals and points was by miniature levers with electro-mechanical interlocking between levers. Multiple-aspect colour-light signals were standardised and full track-circuiting employed. This code of practice remained standard on the Southern for nearly thirty years.

Route Control

The Great Western ventured into power operation although not extensively. In 1927 it introduced one of the pioneer British route-control installations at Newport (Mon). The two station boxes were equipped with route-setting miniature lever frames, although the existing semaphore signals and points, converted to electric operation, were retained. As we have just seen, contemporary power installations followed mechanical practice with one lever controlling one piece of equipment. But power operation provided the opportunity to make one lever control more than one item of equipment—in fact to start a chain reaction through several pieces of equipment. Each lever in the two Newport boxes was made to control a complete route from one stop signal to the next. As in normal semaphore practice a separate signal arm was provided for each diverging route so that in effect there was one lever for every stop signal arm. As the signalman pulled a lever, its stroke was checked in two intermediate positions, first while the equipment proved that the track circuits for the line concerned were clear, and second for the points needed for the route to be

Liverpool Lime Street box installed in 1947 had a miniature-lever frame similar to the type standardised by the Southern Railway. Each lever performed a separate function.

The box at Newport West, Mon, installed in 1927, also employed miniature levers but operating on the route-setting principle. The pulling of one lever set up a complete route from one signal to the next.   [British Railways

correctly set, after which the lever could be pulled fully over to clear the signal. Interlocking between levers was by rotating cams. But the GW did not pursue this idea and although power working was introduced at Paddington, Bristol and Cardiff, individual signal and point levers or handles were used. Nor did the GWR adopt the standard type of multi-aspect colour-light signal, for its colour-light signals showed exactly the same aspects as semaphore stop and distant signals ie red/green, yellow/green, or for a stop and distant together on the same post—red over yellow, green over yellow or double green.

Relay Interlocking—
One Control Switch Operation

The LNER took up the idea in the 1930s of the route-control of signals and points in conjunction with interlocking provided in the electric circuits of the operating controls instead of by mechanical interlocking. Because of this, the principle is usually known as route-relay interlocking. Thus it was no longer necessary for a lever to be used to control an electric contact and initiate a signal or point operation and the way was now open for the use of small thumb switches instead. The thumb switches, mounted in groups on a panel were very much more compact and needed less space than required for a miniature lever frame. Like the GW Newport installation, each switch controlled one route, from one signal to the next. When the switch is operated by turning it through 90 degrees, the electrical equipment proves the route to be free for use, checks that the track circuits are clear, sets or maintains the points concerned in their proper position and clears the signal. As the train passes the signal, it is restored to danger automatically by track circuit occupation, after which the signalman may restore the switch to normal. While the train is still on the portion of line controlled by the switch, track circuit occupation holds the route previously set for the train even though the signal behind the train may be at danger and the thumb switch returned to normal.

The pioneer installation using this system, at Thirsk, was followed by others in the North Eastern area of the LNER at Leeds, Hull and Northallerton. The latter had an important additional feature—the signalman could see the route set up on the signalbox track diagram by a path of illuminated white lights along the tracks concerned. The LNER adopted searchlight colour-light signals for most of its power signalling installations.

At Thirsk the thumb switches, although relatively large by today's standards, were mounted in their geographical positions on the track diagram according to the signal they controlled. In later installations the thumb-switches have been mounted in groups on a desk or console independently of the track diagram. Work on the largest installation of this kind, at York, was started before the last war but was not completed until 1949.

Subsequently this method of operation, known as the OCS (one control switch) system, was adopted on other sections of British Railways, notably for the installations at Glasgow Central (Scottish Region) 1960s scheme, Manchester Piccadilly, Sandbach, Manchester Victoria East and St Pancras (London Midland Region), Newcastle (North Eastern Region), Barnes and Chislehurst Junction (Southern Region). But while these schemes were being

Above: The LMR box at Birmingham New Street, which controls a complex area, has a combined control and indication panel.   *[British Railways*

Below: Manchester Victoria East Junction box has a one-control-switch (OCS) type of panel. The routes set up are displayed by white lights along the tracks concerned on the diagram.

planned or executed, new control techniques in which even smaller control switches or buttons, point, signal and track indications and smaller relays were being developed in conjunction with entrance-exit route control panels.

Relay Interlocking—
Entrance-Exit Panels

The entrance-exit system, for which the pioneer manufacturers, Metropolitan Vickers/GRS, coined the abbreviation the NX system, needs the operation of two switches or buttons to set-up a route, one at the entrance to the route, the other at its exit. Unlike the OCS system there is only one switch or button controlling the entry signal regardless of how many routes it applies to. Each of the routes leading from the signal has an exit button and whichever one is operated in conjunction with the entry switch or button determines the route to be set. The advantage is that the switches and buttons can be mounted geographically on the track diagram, even on a large installation, and the control panel and indications are even more compact than with OCS panels.

The first entrance-exit panel was installed at Brunswick Goods on the Cheshire Lines railway in 1939 but further progress was stopped by the war. The first large installation of this type was brought into service by the Eastern Region in its new box at Stratford during 1949 and entrance-exit panels were standardised for most of the resignalling schemes commissioned as part of the British Railways 1955 modernisation plan.

All the signalling contractors supplying equipment to British Railways during the 1960s manufactured entrance-exit panels. The general principles are similar but they may differ in detail operation. In some there is an entrance switch turned through 90 degrees to initiate a route—in others there is an entrance button which must be depressed to start the sequence, but in both cases there is an exit button which must also be pressed to complete the initiation sequence. On some panels the exit button of one section serves a dual function as the entrance button of the next section ahead. It must therefore be depressed twice—once for each function. Although signalling control panels are made to order for a particular location, one type, produced by the Swiss firm, Integra, and manufactured under licence in Great Britain, and another by Westinghouse, are built up like a mosaic from small rectangular panel sections which plug into a framework. The complete panels are assembled from standard panel components comprising sections for plain track, points, crossings, signals, entrance/exit buttons and so on. The advantage over solid panels is that track alterations after installation can be reproduced easily on the panel by renewing individual panel sections.

The following description of the sequence of operations for setting-up a route on an entrance-exit panel makes an interesting comparison with the block signalling sequence. The signalman first momentarily presses the button opposite the signal for the route he wishes to clear; this action sets a white light flashing within the button. He then momentarily presses the button at the end of the route he requires to be set up; provided the route is free to be used, this action initiates the route-setting process. If the signalling controls are free, points are moved to the required position and locked; or, if they are already

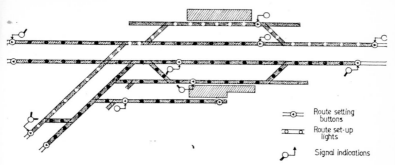

Route setting buttons

Route set-up lights

Signal indications

FIG 35 Diagram illustrating the principal features of an entrance-exit signalling control panel.

correctly set, they will be locked in the position in which they lie. As points become locked in the correct position, a line of small white lights is illuminated along the route concerned on the track diagram and the flashing white light in the entry button becomes steady. These lights are known as route lights and confirm to the signalman that the route has successfully been established and locked. Finally, after the route is proved, the signal will clear and its red indication on the panel changes to green, showing the signalman that the signal is displaying a proceed indication. (The signal repeater on the panel shows green though the signal itself may be displaying yellow or double yellow). The whole operation from the depression of the first entrance button to the clearing of the signal may take from one to several seconds.

The passage of the train is shown on the diagram by the route lights of the track circuits concerned changing from white to red. After the train has passed, the signal returns automatically to red and the route can be cancelled by the signalman momentarily pulling out the relevant entrance button, which extinguishes the route lights after they have reverted to white following a track-circuit occupied indication. Should the signalman fail to restore the route after a train (where required to do so), the white route lights remain illuminated as a reminder to him. Once a signal has been cleared, the signalman cannot change the route until the train has passed or unless a two-minute time release period has elapsed. He can immediately restore a signal for a route set in error by pulling up the entrance button, but cannot set a new route until the time release period has expired. When the time release is used, a flashing red light in the panel signal indication reminds the signalman of the situation.

To minimise demands on the signalman, the action of restoring a route after the passage of a train is obviated wherever possible. Many controlled signals frequently required for successive trains can be arranged to work automatically, once the entrance and exit buttons have been operated, by the pressing of an adjoining auto button, until the signalman wishes to set up an alternative route or hold the signal at red; in the latter event he pulls out the auto button to cancel automatic working.

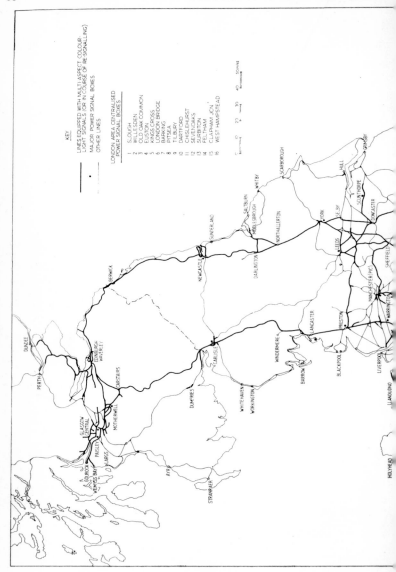

KEY

LINES EQUIPPED WITH MULTI-ASPECT COLOUR-
LIGHT SIGNALS (OR IN COURSE OF RE-SIGNALLING)

MAJOR POWER SIGNAL BOXES

OTHER LINES

LONDON AREA & CENTRALISED
POWER SIGNAL BOXES

1 — SLOUGH
2 — WILLESDEN
3 — OLD OAK COMMON
4 — EUSTON
5 — KINGS CROSS
6 — LONDON BRIDGE
7 — BARKING
8 — PITSEA
9 — TILBURY
10 — DARTFORD
11 — CHISLEHURST
12 — SEVENOAKS
13 — SURBITON
14 — FELTHAM
15 — CLAPHAM JCN
16 — WEST HAMPSTEAD

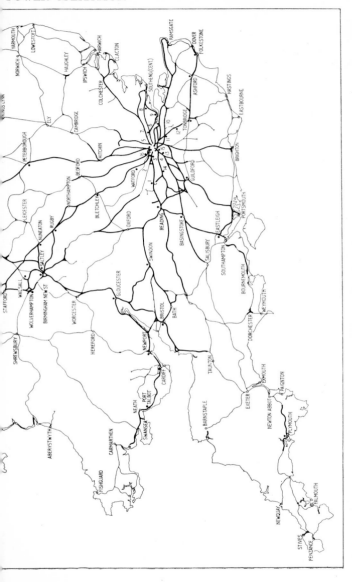

FIG 36 Map showing BR routes with multiple-aspect signalling, together with major centralised power signalboxes, including conversions in hand but not complete, at the beginning of 1978.

Above: One of the first stretches of automatic signalling was installed on the LSWR between Woking and Basingstoke in the early years of the present century and lasted until 1966. The photograph shows the original painting of the distant arms and the Coligny-Welch indicators alongside the distant spectacle plates.   [*British Railways*

Below: The interior of London Bridge 1928 signal box SR showing the miniature lever frame and the rotary clock-type train describers.   [*British Railways*

Route pre-selection facilities are not provided, but on some panels routes governed by certain controlled signals, which the operating authorities deem undesirable for automatic working, may be pre-set for a second identical move before the previous train is clear. To permit pre-setting, special control features allow the signalman to operate the route buttons for a second movement over the same route as soon as the passage of the first train has placed the signal governing the route to danger. The signal for the second move will clear only when the route is free for it to do so.

Independent point-operating buttons or switches are provided to permit individual operation of a pair of points should the need arise, provided that the points are not locked by a route set through them. The point-operating switches must usually be returned to their normal central or neutral position before a subsequent route can be set up through the points concerned. White repeater lights alongside each operating switch show the lie of the points; an illuminated F or other indication shows whether they are free or route locked. In some cases the signalman can alter the position of points by the individual point switch or special overlap keys to obtain an alternative overlap beyond a signal where the normal overlap is occupied.

Between the controlled junctions are many miles of automatic signals. Although automatic signals are not controlled from a signal cabin they are often supervised by the signalman at the next signalbox ahead, for his track diagram generally shows the state of the track circuit sections and repeats the signal aspects of all the automatic sections on the lines approaching his signal cabin. He is not usually interested in trains which have passed beyond his last controlled signal section. In the latest installations the division between powerbox control areas is basically geographical. Signal post telephones are provided at every automatic signal and controlled running signal to permit train crews to talk to the signalman supervising the section when needed.

Because trains on many main lines with modern signalling now run long distances without being observed directly by signalmen, hot axlebox detectors are installed at strategic locations on lines controlled from centralised power-boxes. The lineside equipment is linked to signalbox recording apparatus which sounds an alarm and shows the location of up to four overheated axleboxes in a passing train. The signalman can then stop the train and arrange to have it inspected.

Single lines have also benefited from modern power installations but not to the same extent, for few British Railways single lines carry an amount of traffic sufficient to justify the expense of such resignalling. A form of direction lever working has been installed on some lines and has been adapted in at least one power installation and controlled by entrance-exit type push buttons.

Remote Control

In modern centralised power signalling installations the large control areas have only become possible by modern developments in electronic remote control systems. Interlocking between signals and points and between conflicting routes in modern signalling is carried out by conventional signalling relays which switch electric circuits to ensure that signals cannot be cleared unless the route is correctly set and that no other train is in the way. Interlocking relays are housed in relay rooms located at major junctions near the points and signals they control. The signalbox control panel may, however, be many miles away. The link between the control panel and the relay room might be by direct wire in the case of distances up to about five miles, with separate wire pairs for each piece of equipment. Beyond this distance remote control systems are used in which one pair of wires is capable of carrying commands and indications for several pieces of equipment. This is achieved either by a time division multiplex (tdm) system in which synchronised scanning equipment at each end of the remote control link scans the input circuits of each item of equipment in turn several times a second and if a change is detected it will register on the corresponding equipment at the other end, or by frequency division multiplex (fdm) in which coded signals at different frequencies can be transmitted over one circuit simultaneously. Some of the larger power signalboxes control up to a dozen or so remote relay interlockings in this way. Two large centralised power boxes on BR, Trent and Saltley, have all the relay interlocking equipment within the main signalbox and links to signals and points are carried by fdm equipment designed to avoid any possibility of false operation. There are advantages and disadvantages in this system and all subsequent power box schemes have had separate remote-controlled relay rooms.

Track Circuit Block

The earliest power installations at principal stations were self-contained and covered only the station and its immediate approaches. Later schemes were more extensive and covered longer sections of line. Power signalboxes control junctions and associated signals but between the controlled areas the signals work automatically, and are operated only by the passage of trains occupying and clearing track circuits. Automatic signalling is not new, for the London & South Western Railway installed automatic semaphore signals, governed by track circuits, on its main line between Woking and Basingstoke with controlled signals at intermediate stations, in 1902. The low pressure pneumatic system was used to work the signal arms. Most signals had stop and distant arms and thus the system was similar in effect to modern three-aspect colour-light schemes. The system remained in use until 1966 but was then renewed with colour-light signals. Automatic signals normally showed clear and only returned to danger behind a train until it passed beyond the overlap of the signal ahead, a practice followed today with automatic colour-light signals. Controlled signals on the other hand were normally at danger and only cleared for the passage of a train. The first automatic multiple-aspect colour-light signals on a main line were installed between Neasden and Marylebone in 1923.

FIG 37 Track circuit indications of an automatic section are displayed on the track diagram at the next signal box ahead.

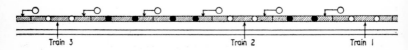

The electrification of the London-Brighton line in 1932 and the associated resignalling was one of the earliest examples of the conversion of long lengths of main line to power signalling. At that time it was not a complete conversion, for several mechanical signalboxes were retained but adapted for power signalling, and mechanically-worked semaphore signalling remained in operation at the London end of the line for another 20 years, but it set the pattern for the future.

The extensive signalling modernisation programme initiated in the mid-1950s which gathered momentum with resignalling for new electrification around London and Glasgow, and on the Southern Region between 1959 and 1962, the progressive conversion of the main Western Region routes from 1958 which continues today, the wholesale conversion of the West Coast main line between London, Liverpool, Manchester, and Glasgow as part of the vast main line electrification scheme, and major pro ects at centres on the Eastern Region, has virtually brought the elimination of old type mechanical signalling and manual block working on most principal British Railways main lines. Indeed by 1973 modern signalling, with multiple-aspect signals, continuous track circuiting, the automatic track to train warning system (aws), and control from (mostly) large centralised power signalboxes, known by the generic term track circuit block (tcb), extended unbrokenly on lines bounded by Paddington, Bristol, Taunton, to the outskirts of Swansea, from Bristol to Birmingham, Derby, Nottingham, Sheffield and Leeds and from Euston to Glasgow. The longest continuous length of tcb extends from Taunton via Bristol and Birmingham to Glasgow, a distance of about 430 miles. At the beginning of 1977 10,094 single track miles on BR were equipped with colour-light signalling out of a total mileage of 22,401. This figure takes into account the completion of the powerboxes at Warrington, Preston, Carlisle and Motherwell which has added about 900 miles.

Other schemes now in hand as this edition closes for press will provide continuous mas from Kings Cross power signalbox to Peterborough, Doncaster, Sheffield, Leeds, York, Newcastle and Edinburgh. The Western Region meanwhile is planning or undertaking extensions which will take tcb to the west of Swansea, from Reading via the Berks & Hants line to Taunton and on from there through Exeter to link with the existing power signalbox at Plymouth. The map on pages 80-1 shows the extent of tcb as at the beginning of 1978.

Train Describers

In all forms of railway signalling the signalman must know when a train is approaching him and, at a junction or station, must also know in advance the type of train and its destination so that he can set the correct route. In areas worked by the block telegraph system, the Is line clear? bell code not only warns him that a train is approaching but also tells him the type of train. His timetable tells him where the train is going, but if trains are out of order the signalman in the next box will telephone telling him what train is coming.

In small power installations, block working is often maintained with adjacent boxes or, if full track circuiting is provided, the single stroke block bell is used instead as a train describer bell. Trains are not offered and accepted but are merely belled on by the appropriate Is line clear? bell code. But something more is required in the larger power installations, particularly where there are

UP LINE		1	2	3
1	CANCEL	●	●	●
2	Via SV FAST PASS.	●	●	○
3	Via SV SEMI. PASS.	●	●	●
4	Via SV STPG. PASS.	●	○	●
5	Via SV E/V/E	●	●	●
6	Via SV · FT.	○	●	●
7	Via PENS. PASS.	●	●	●

FIG 38   A detail portion of a magazine train describer used by the Southern Region which indicates first, second and third train approaching by a light opposite the description.

several automatic sections between controlled areas, for a signalman could not be expected to remember the descriptions of several trains approaching him at the same time. The signalman knows when trains approach him by the indications on the track circuit diagram. He knows the type and destination from the train describer. Earlier patterns comprise a small cabinet with a vertical list of printed train types and destinations. Alongside each description is a push button and lamp or, in some describers, three lamps. To set the describer the signalman simply presses the button alongside the appropriate description. When the train passes a given point the description is transmitted automatically to the receiver instrument at the box ahead where the light is illuminated alongside the description concerned. Some instruments can display up to three trains approaching—1st, 2nd and 3rd—and most describers have storage facilities for additional descriptions of following trains. Sometimes when the train arrives the description is automatically removed from the describer, but in others the signalman must manually remove the description by operating a clear description button. As the train passes he must of course re-describe the train forward in the describer to the next box. The signalman at the transmitting describer has a last train sent indication which remains illuminated until he sets a fresh description.

But this describer, at one time the Southern Region standard, has been superseded by automatic describers which, once set, depend entirely on train movement for the transmission of the description. One of the first types of automatic train describer was installed at signalboxes between Liverpool Street and Shenfield in conjunction with the 1949 electrification scheme. The describers in each cabin consist of a number of panels, one for each line. Each panel consists of several apertures corresponding to a section of track at specified

Train describers: Above is the stencil type as used at Weaver Junction LMR; *above right* the standard SR pattern as used at Tonbridge in which the type of train and its destination are described. *Right:* For all but the earliest of the 1950s and 1960s resignalling schemes and excepting the Western Region, BR adopted train describers with cathode-ray tube (crt) displays on the track diagram. This is a part of Warrington panel. *Below:* The Western Region uses a rotating counter display for train description on a separate diagram in all its power signalling schemes, including this one at Reading. [*Westinghouse Brake and Signal Co (right); British Railways*

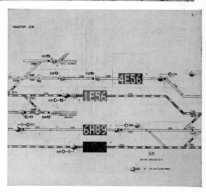

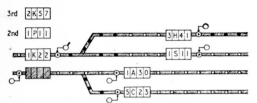

FIG 39 Train describers in recent installations are incorporated in the track diagram in the signal box control panel.

signals. The train description is given by code letters indicating class and destination which are illuminated in the apertures. The signalman at the starting station sets up the code on his describer by operating push buttons, after which the description is passed forward from describer to describer by track circuit occupation as the train proceeds on its journey. While in the area controlled by a signal cabin the description code is displayed in each aperture in turn corresponding to the signals for the line on which the train is running. If the train is signalled to cross from slow to fast lines or to a branch route the description is transferred automatically from the slow to fast line (or branch) describer without any action by the signalman.

This principle has been continued in the latest power installations, but the advances in design and, particularly, miniaturisation, in recent years have permitted the production of more compact describers. Most of the recent installations have the train describer apertures, which are related to signal sections, displayed in their appropriate geographical positions on a track diagram either on a separate panel at the back of the signal control console or incorporated in the actual control panel. Most of the new describers display the four-character codes formerly used as train headcodes. The codes indicate the train classification, the destination area and the train number or in the case of local trains, a route number. Thus the signalman not only can see by track circuit indications all the trains in the area he controls or supervises, he also knows the identity of every train by the train describer code.

If trains start or terminate on lines controlled by intermediate signal cabins the signalman has facilities to insert or delete the descriptions of the trains concerned. The codes on the latest describers are usually set up by push buttons but on the Western Region, telephone-type dials are used instead. The actual descriptions are shown by one of four types of display—stencil type, rotating counter, edge-lit engraved Perspex or cathode tube. Mechanical signalboxes on

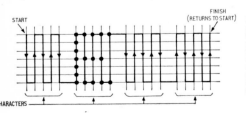

FIG 40 The characters on a crt train describer display are formed on a 5 by 7 matrix in which only the dots at the intersections required for the character are visible. The electron beam brights-up the appropriate dots to make the characters visible as it passes across the tube.

the fringe of a power-controlled area may be equipped with a small control panel, and perhaps a train describer to signal trains to and from a main power box, but retain levers and block instruments for working in the opposite direction.

Although various types of four-character train describer display were employed in the early centralised power signalboxes as part of the progressive signalling modernisation programme commissioned during the early 1960s cathode ray tube (crt) displays have been standardised in the latest installations. Moreover in signalboxes opened from the early 1970s—for example Dartford, Warrington, Preston, Carlisle, Motherwell and Glasgow Central—computers are employed for the heart of the train describer system. The computer memory store is fed with details of train movements from track circuit occupation and inward descriptions from adjacent signalboxes or set-up within the controlling signalbox, from which it produces the train describer displays on the signalling console. This in itself is no more than is done by earlier types of describer equipment. Computer-based describers have additional facilities; for example in certain types of failure involving a momentary loss of power the computer memory can recall the panel displays which is not possible on the older types. The computer can also be interrogated on the whereabouts of trains. For example signalbox supervisory staff who wish to locate a train can feed in an enquiry quoting the train reporting number and the computer will print out the signal location of the train if it is within the area of that box. It can provide a track diagram on a visual display unit (vdu). See page 130. Moreover the computer can provide automatic print-outs of train passing times at selected locations as a record of train running. Where regular services run to a similar pattern recorded train announcements and platform visual indicators can be triggered off by the computer when it receives given train descriptions at specified locations. Normally two computers are provided, sometimes with one dealing with up trains and the other down trains but both having capacity to take over the full service in the event of a failure of one of them.

Level Crossings

Level crossings in power signalled areas can be controlled from a signalbox or from a mechanical gate box. The gate box lever frame may be released from a switch on the power box panel or, if it is in a section controlled by automatic colour light signals, the gate box may have a track circuit indicator and/or bell warning signal to show when trains are approaching. Usually in this case the gate box will have signal levers to control the colour light signals at the approach to the crossing and the signals must first be placed at danger before the gates are opened to road traffic. The gate keeper must ensure that he doesn't place the signals at danger in the face of an approaching train. If he does, perhaps in an emergency, a time delay prevents him from opening the gates to road traffic immediately.

In recent years several new types of level crossing protection have been evolved for use on BR, particularly in the adoption of lifting barriers to replace gates, for they are cheaper to instal and maintain and allow for easier operation. In some cases they are full barriers, that is barriers which close completely across the road; although they are power operated they are worked from a signalbox and interlocked with the signals in the usual way.

G

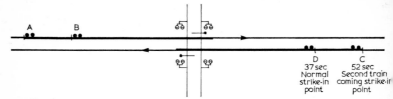

FIG 41 Track circuit and treadle arrangement at automatic half-barrier level crossing.
Treadles B and D mark the normal strike-in point for the first train, while A and C are for a
second train to hold the barriers down if it will reach the crossing less than 15 sec after the
first clears the crossing.

Elsewhere automatic half-barrier crossings have been provided on lines in
power or manually signalled areas. The barriers themselves lower across the
left half of the road on the approach to the crossing, the exit from the crossing
being left open. They are controlled automatically by an approaching train.
The original specification and installation programme was halted following the
collision between an electrically-hauled express train travelling at about 75 mph
and a slow moving road transporter carrying an exceptional load at Hixon crossing in January 1968. Following the public inquiry revised regulations were
instituted which made the cost savings over manned crossings less attractive
because of the increased track operating distance some crossings planned for
conversion to ahb operation could not in fact be converted since signalling
complications at nearby stations or junctions would have interfered with the
timing sequence or would have been too costly.

The operating sequence of ahbs is controlled by approach track circuits and
treadles on both tracks or in both directions on single lines. Both forms of
equipment are provided to eliminate any possibility of failure, and are located
in a position to give minimum times from the start of the timing sequence to
the arrival of the fastest train travelling at line speed. All crossings are equipped
with road signals to control road vehicles but are not specifically protected by
rail signals. Railway signals might be sited in the approach control area of a
crossing in which case the signal circuits will be linked to the crossing so that
the barrier lowering sequence will not operate if the signal is at danger but
starts before the signal clears.

When no trains are in the vicinity the road traffic lights are out. As a train
approaches and strikes in at the approach track circuit and treadle to start the
timing sequence a loud bell starts to ring, the traffic lights first show a steady
amber for 5 seconds to warn road vehicles as in the normal traffic light sequence,
followed by a pair of flashing red lights; a few seconds later the barriers lower
across the road. The bell stops but the lights continue to flash. The minimum
time from the moment the fastest train strikes in to its arrival at the crossing is
37 seconds. In some cases where train speeds vary widely speed measuring
equipment is employed to detect whether a fast express passenger train or
slower moving freight train is approaching and the fall of the barriers is adjusted
automatically. As the last coach or wagon clears the crossing the barriers lift
and the red lights cease to flash unless a second train is approaching on the
opposite line. If a second train will reach the strike-in point on the opposite line

less than 15 seconds after the first train strikes out the barriers remain lowered, the red lights continue to flash and a second train coming indicator is illuminated. This procedure is to ensure that the barriers do not start to rise with slow moving traffic starting away as the sequence restarts almost immediately for the second train.

Telephones are provided at all ahb crossings for use by drivers of slow moving or long road vehicles who are required to ask the permission of the signalman in the supervising signalbox before they drive over the crossing. After they have driven across they must telephone again to advise the signalman that their vehicle is clear.

Some crossings because of traffic density or location are not suitable for ahbs and other methods of remote operation have been tried. One which is gradually being adopted is manual remote control from a signalbox or crossing cabin with visual supervision by closed circuit television. In this way centralised power signalboxes or mechanical signalboxes can work crossings some distance away although the number worked in this manner from one location is limited. In some instances a group of closely spaced crossings in say a town may be worked by one crossing keeper located at one of the crossings. Normally these remote crossings are operated electrically through push button control panels.

Another type of crossing protection installed on little-used roads employs swing gates which open away from the railway and are operated by the road user; small red and green warning lights indicate to the road user whether or not a train is approaching. When both the approach track circuits are clear a green light is displayed, but if a train is approaching a red light warns the road user that he must not move on to the crossing. It is essential for the user to open the far gate first, then the near gate before driving over the railway. Some crossings of this type have been equipped with hydraulically-powered lifting barriers which are raised by road users operating a pump. After crossing, the road user releases the hydraulic controls and the barriers fall. With this type of barrier the road user only passes over the crossing once instead of five times needed with swing gates.

Another innovation introduced in recent years is an open crossing used on single lines, without gates or barriers; train speed is limited to 10mph. In some instances the train is required to stop before reaching the crossing and whistle before proceeding. In other cases red flashing lights are provided for road users, initiated either by track circuit occupation or by the operation of a plunger by the train driver at a stop board. Trains using open crossings at night must carry searchlight headlights.

Ground Frames

As in mechanical areas, little-used intermediate sidings on main lines do not justify the expense of providing remotely worked points and associated signalling equipment and they are, therefore, controlled from ground frames at the site. The ground frame may be released by a switch on the panel of the nearest power signal cabin but, where the line is fully track-circuited, other methods may be used. Usually, remote sidings are served only by local freight trains, perhaps shunting two or three wagons in and taking out two or three others, while the rest of the train stands on the main line. In this case the train itself

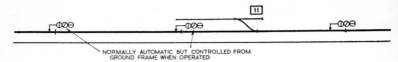

NORMALLY AUTOMATIC BUT CONTROLLED FROM
GROUND FRAME WHEN OPERATED

FIG 42   A ground frame controlling a siding in an automatically signalled section.

may release the ground frame by what is known as split train track circuit control.
While the train is shunting and the ground frame in use the semi-automatic
signal in the rear is held at danger.

On some lines the ground frames in automatic sections are released by a
special release key which is inserted into the locking lever. Signal levers may be
provided on the ground frame to control automatic signals in the vicinity
where necessary. Trains may be shunted clear of the main lines at these locations, after which the ground frame is restored to normal for automatic through
working. When shunting is complete the shunter or guard must telephone to
the signalman at the supervising box for permission to let the train out on
to the main line again, not to obtain a release, for that is given by the key in his
possession, but to ensure that a more important train is not delayed.

7—Automatic Warning Systems and Automatic Train Control

From the early days of railways, engineers had experimented with forms of
automatic train control in an endeavour to produce audible or visual signals
in a locomotive cab in conjunction with or instead of ordinary lineside signals.
Some were more ambitious and incorporated automatic stop devices which
operated if a train passed a signal at danger. Many experiments were unsuccessful but by the time the four railway companies were nationalised in 1948, two
had developed reliable forms of automatic warning systems, in everyday service.
The system in use on the Great Western Railway employed mechanical contact
between a shoe on the locomotive and a track ramp. That on the Fenchurch
Street-Shoeburyness line of the LMS employed the Hudd magnetic induction
system, with no physical contact between the track apparatus and the receiver
on the locomotive. Both types were used at distant signals and gave the driver
an audible indication of the position of the signal. After many very thorough
tests and experiments had been carried out, a new system was evolved for use
as a standard on BR which employs magnetic induction and a visual indicator
like the Hudd system, and the audible warnings of the GW system. The BR
standard automatic warning system (aws) is being installed as rapidly as possible
on all regions, and on the Western, has replaced the former GW electro-
mechanical system.

The system is designed to assist the driver in the working of his train, especially
in adverse weather conditions, when signals may be difficult to observe. Where
aws is installed, two track magnets are placed longitudinally between the
running rails, approximately 200yd on the approach side of distant signals

The interior of a cab fitted with BR aws. Note the spoked wheel pattern on the visual indicator which is displayed after a caution indication has been acknowledged by the driver.

[*British Railways*

The first magnet is a permanent magnet inductor, the second an electro-magnet inductor. The electro-magnet inductor is energised only when the distant signal is cleared, and in semaphore areas, the circuit is proved through both the signal arm and its lever in the signalbox. In colour-light areas all running signals normally have aws magnets; the electro-magnet is energised only when a green, clear, indication is displayed and caution is given in the cab for red, yellow, or double yellow.

A receiver is mounted on the locomotive or multiple-unit, generally underneath the leading bogie; it is so placed that it passes directly over the magnets, with a 5in clear space between. In the cab are a bell, a horn and a visual indicator with a cancelling handle. This indicator shows either a black face or a vivid yellow and black circular spoked pattern. When a locomotive approaches the aws magnets the receiver on the locomotive first passes over the permanent magnet inductor and this trips the receiver.

If the distant signal is at caution the electro-magnet inductor is not energised, and after a one second delay, the horn sounds. The driver acknowledges this warning with the resetting handle, and this action turns the visual indicator to the yellow and black spoke pattern, this display remaining as a reminder to the driver that he has cancelled a caution warning until the next distant signal aws magnet is passed when the all-black indication is restored. If this signal is also at caution, when the driver cancels the warning, the yellow/black spokes re-appear, for each indication must be separately cancelled, and the driver cannot forestall the indication. If the driver does not cancel the warning, a

BR standard magnetic aws magnets. The unit nearer the camera is the permanent magnet which initiates the warning and braking sequence on a train, while the far unit is the electro-magnet, energised only when the related signal is at green (or semaphore distant clear) to counteract the warning sequence and provide the bell indication on the train.

[*British Railways*

brake application starts automatically, bringing the train to a stop.

If the distant signal is clear, the second, electro-magnet inductor will be energised. This resets the receiver and gives a two-second ring on the bell in the cab. The one-second delay on the circuit allows a clear indication to be given even at speeds as low as 1¾mph. At a lower speed than this a warning will be given even if the signal is off. When a signal is at clear, there is no indication on the visual indicator, which remains all-black.

Where aws is installed on single lines with bi-directional running and signalling, it is obviously undesirable for trains travelling in one direction to receive indications applicable to trains travelling in the other. To prevent the unrequired permanent inductors tripping the locomotive gear, suppressor inductors of considerable power are installed adjacent to the track magnets.

Cab Signalling and Automatic Driving Systems

For higher speeds of the future and to provide a more positive indication than can be given by simple aws on BR for multiple-aspect signalling systems, British Railways and other overseas railway administrations are experimenting with various forms of cab signalling. In this branch of signalling British Railways can no longer afford to work alone as the possibility of a Channel Tunnel still being planned would mean that the BR system is no longer physically isolated from the European rail network. While through working by motive power is likely to be confined to set train formations on high speed passenger services between London and Paris/Brussels, the Channel Tunnel approach lines may well be used by other services which will need to be compatible with any sophisticated automated signalling used on Channel Tunnel lines to obtain full benefits. Thus while the BR research department is conducting trials with forms of cab signalling of its own development, at the time this edition went to press a French-designed cab signalling and track circuit system was under evaluation on a section of the Fenchurch Street-Southend line.

Two basic forms of track equipment are used for cab signalling. One employs the normal running rails for transmission of coded currents detected by pick-up coils on the train. The second type uses independent track conductors formed usually by pairs of cables running a specified distance apart along the centre of the track. Again pick up coils on the train detect the coded currents carried by the conductors. The two systems have a number of advantages and disadvantages. Independent conductors are more costly but are capable of providing more functions than running-rail coded track circuits. By transposing track conductor loops over each other at for example 100 metre intervals train speed can be measured by lineside apparatus and train borne equipment can measure precisely distance travelled. Moreover, various means of communication between track and train can be provided, for example speech circuits between train operator and central control, data transmission of driving commands or instructions and measurement of train performance, and in highly sophisticated systems fully automated driving control. London Transport using running rails for carrying coded signals already has its automated Victoria Line described on page 116.

The British Railways research programme has two experimental cab signalling installations under evaluation in line service, one at Wilmslow on the LMR ac electrified line, and the other on parts of the Southern Region's dc third rail electrified Waterloo-Bournemouth line. The two systems are related since they form part of the same line of experiment. The project has been broken down into sub systems since all the track-train communication facilities capable of being transmitted may not be justified for every section of line, or for all types of train. Thus the Southern Region trial consists only of intermittent cab signalling equipment capable of displaying the aspect of the next signal ahead from a point about 200 metres before the train reaches the signal and showing the aspect of the signal that it has passed until it reaches the approach indication of the following signal. This is achieved by a combination of the standard aws track permanent magnet as in simple aws, but instead of the electro-magnet energised if the signal ahead is clear there is a 200-250 metre length of track conductor from the permanent magnet to the signal which by high frequency codes transmitted to the train produces the appropriate signal aspect on the driver's display unit. The permanent magnet on the track starts an automatic braking sequence on every occasion but if the signal to which it relates is at green the coded currents in the track conductor loop automatically cancel the

FIG 43 Layout of signals, aws permanent magnet and track conductor cable loop from the transmitter of the signal repeating automatic warning system on trial on the SR.

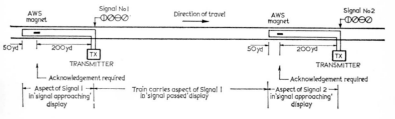

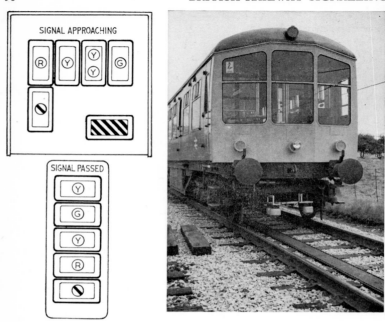

Above left: **FIG 44** The cab display of signal repeating aws; at the top are the driver's acknowledgement buttons. *Above right:* BR's battery powered test train on the Derby Friargate line used for experiments in train control systems. [*British Railways*

brake application through the trainborne equipment. For any other aspect the braking sequence can only be cancelled by the driver pressing the acknowledgment button of the signal aspect concerned. If he fails to press the acknowledgement button or presses the wrong one the braking sequence takes effect within a few seconds and brings the train to a halt. The system also has a trip effect in-built so that if a train approaches a red signal which the driver duly acknowledges, but fails to stop at the signal an emergency brake application is made automatically. When a proceed aspect is displayed, as the train passes the signal and runs off the track conductor the signal aspect is transferred from the signal approaching to the signal passed display as a reminder of the last signal, until the train reaches the next permanent magnet and track conductor at the signal ahead. This is an intermittent system since information is only being transmitted to the train for the 250 metres approaching a signal. It is known by the initials sraws—signal repeating automatic warning system.

The Wilmslow installation (and the BR research section's own branch line near Derby—the former GNR Derby Friargate line) is an expansion of the Southern Region type to a continuous cab signalling system including continuous indication of permitted speed and comparison of actual speed. The trainborne

Driver's display unit used in BR train control experiments. The top band represents actual train speed, the second band permissible speed, and the bottom band the target distance to a change of condition, for example a speed restriction.

[*British Railways*

equipment is centred round a computer which is programmed with the train's characteristics, and such physical details of the line as curves, gradients, distance to next signal or to speed restrictions are fed in from track equipment at appropriate locations so that braking distance can be established and presented to the driver as a speed instruction. Two-way speech communication and other facilities can also be provided. The advantage of this system is that the whole package does not have to be provided in one go and can be built up piece by piece as required or in accordance with financial justification. Ultimately the system would be capable of fully automated driving control.

The sraws is unlikely to be installed generally though, whatever its advantages, on grounds of cost. Another form of track/train communication—transponders—is being installed on the West Coast main line. See page 129.

Trip Apparatus

Another form of automatic train control is the trip arm system. Unlike the automatic warning system, however, this system is applied to stop signals, and positively stops any train which is tripped. A trip arm is mounted on the track beside every stop signal equipped with the system. It is fixed on the sleeper ends parallel to the running rails, and at the same height. When the signal is clear the trip arm lies in a horizontal position, below rail level, and trains can pass freely. When the signal is at danger the arm is raised to the vertical position above rail level, either electrically or pneumatically. If a train approaches a signal at danger and correctly stops at the signal, nothing happens until the signal clears, when the trip arm lowers and the train may proceed unhindered.

If the train attempts to pass a signal at danger, however, the trip arm comes into contact with a trip lever mounted low on the frame of the locomotive or motor coach. The trip lever is thus deflected and operates a valve connected to the brake system which releases air to the atmosphere, thus applying the brakes on the train. It is thus impossible for a train to pass a signal at danger without being tripped and brought to a stand. The driver must then reset the trip arm before the brakes can be released, and the possibility of a driver inadvertently running past a signal at danger is eliminated. The system has not been generally adopted but is used on London Transport lines, the SR Waterloo & City tube and LMR Euston-Watford and Liverpool Central-Birkenhead electrified lines.

8—Emergency Working

However good the organisation of a railway there are always some incidents which interrupt the smooth working of the train service. Some are due to freaks of chance that usually occur at most awkward times, others perhaps to carelessness or disregard of rules on the part of staff, while some are attributable to the actions of passengers. There may be a derailment, perhaps a wagon that jumps the track in a siding during shunting and tilts towards the main line; a herd of cattle may break through a fence and take a stroll on the line; or a signalman may see a passenger train pass by with a door swinging open on one of the coaches; a passenger may pull the alarm signal and the train stops two or three miles from a station; in the extreme, and fortunately rarely, there may be a major accident. All are unplanned incidents so far as timetables are concerned, but all fall within the category of emergency working, for which prescribed routines covering all anticipated types of incident lay down exactly what steps the signalmen and train crews must take, firstly to ensure the safety of trains and secondly to keep the traffic moving either partially or fully. In some instances, interruptions to services may be planned in advance. The engineer's department may have to re-lay track, or renew a bridge, in which case special measures are taken to ensure the safety of the men and machines on the line and for the working of trains, which may have to run in both directions over a single line of what is normally a double-track section.

Many of the emergency procedures have been evolved and maintained from the earliest days of railways and certainly since the establishment of the block system decreed by law in 1889. During the 1960s and 1970s with the replacement of mechanical signalling by large areas of track circuit block controlled by centralised power signalboxes some emergency procedures were rendered obsolete because special moves now came within the jurisdiction of one signalman or became incapable of observance as originally laid down because a modern signalbox may be many miles away with only telephone communication between signalman and train crew. Nevertheless emergency procedures devised for mechanically-signalled lines with relatively closely-spaced signalboxes are still employed on lines retaining this form of signalling and are described here with the principal variations for track circuit block lines.

Detonators

A detonator is an audible signal; it is clipped to the top of the rail usually by hand and when an engine or coach wheel passes over it, the detonator explodes with a sharp bang, for it must be heard on a locomotive above the sounds of the locomotive itself. Generally speaking, detonators are used to attract drivers' attention to unusual or special working affecting the line over which they are running. Many signalboxes are equipped with lever operated detonator placers for use in an emergency or during fog.

If at any time a running line becomes obstructed by a disabled train outside the protection of the normal signals, that is within a block section, the train must be protected. The standard method of protection is by detonators, which are placed on the line or lines affected—one at $\frac{1}{4}$ mile, one at $\frac{1}{2}$ mile and three,

20yd apart, one mile from the obstruction, duplicated on both rails on IC 125 routes.

Detonators are also used to protect planned obstructions such as engineering works, where machines are in use, or where the track has been removed. A crane relaying track may turn intermittently and foul a line in use for traffic. In this case a handsignalman protects the crane on the line in use by trains. He is stationed one mile, or even more depending on location, from the obstruction and places three detonators 20yd apart on the rail of the track concerned and exhibits a red handsignal (flag by day, lamp by night) so that an approaching train will have ample time to stop before the site of the works is reached. A second handsignalman will usually be stationed close to the obstruction so that when the crane or other equipment is clear of the line in use, this handsignalman can authorise the train to proceed by displaying a green handsignal. Where engineering works take place near a signalbox and partially or fully within station limits, handsignalmen and detonators may or may not be used in conjunction with the normal signalling—it depends on the location and the type of work.

As described in the section on working during fog, detonators are used singly to denote a semaphore signal at danger or caution. The detonators are placed on the line by fogsignalmen allocated to specified signals.

Protection

In the event of an accident or an incident of any sort, any line that becomes obstructed must be protected promptly, first by a track circuit clip being placed across the rails (except on lines electrified on the third rail system) and then by detonator protection, as just described, in the direction from which trains approach. It is vital that obstructed adjoining lines carrying trains in the opposite or same direction are protected even before the track on which the disabled train is standing, since while in theory a second train should not immediately approach on the line occupied by the disabled train because it is protected by the block system or track circuit block, it is quite possible for a train to approach on another line if it has already passed the last controlled signal before the signalman concerned has been told of the accident. With line speeds of 100mph or more an approaching train might be 10 miles away when an accident occurs which fouls its track, yet the train crew carrying out protection have only a few seconds over four minutes in which to carry out protection and advise the controlling signalman in order to give the approaching train adequate emergency braking distance to stop before running into the obstruction. This is where vital

FIG 45   Protection by track circuit clip and detonators of a disabled train. The adjacent and opposite tracks are protected if they are obstructed in any way.

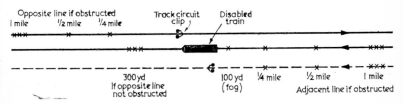

seconds count in applying a track circuit clip which should afford immediate first stage protection on track circuited lines.

If the train has been stopped by mishap the guard and driver (or secondman if the cab is double-manned) walk towards each other on the off side of the train, unless the guard is riding on the locomotive, in which case they confer immediately to ascertain whether any other line is obstructed. If it is, protection must be carried out promptly with track circuit clips and detonators as just described. The guard walks back to protect the train and any other obstructed line carrying traffic in the same direction. In fog an extra detonator is put down 100yd behind the failed train. Meanwhile the driver (or secondman) goes forward to carry out protection of lines carrying trains in the opposite direction. If the driver or guard reaches a telephone, for example at a signal, he must use it to inform the signalman of the incident and what assistance and medical help may be needed.

If the train stops because of a failure and not an accident and no other line is obstructed, the failed train must still be protected. The driver (or secondman) puts down three detonators 20yd apart 300yd ahead of the failure on the same line, in case assistance comes from ahead as described in the section on wrong direction movements.

Clearly in the case of a major accident when one or more of the train crew may be injured, remaining fit train staff must do their best in the circumstances, protecting opposite lines first. If on the other hand the train has stopped because the alarm signal has been operated by a passenger and no other line is obstructed, if the train cannot restart immediately the driver (secondman if the locomotive is double-manned) goes back to protect the rear while the guard attends to the passenger concerned.

Wrong Direction Movements

Trains must normally work over a line only in the right direction. In cases of emergency it may become necessary for trains to work in the wrong direction, that is against the normal flow of traffic for the line in question. Unless special signalling is installed, as on ordinary single lines or where signalling has been provided for both-ways working, for example at or near certain important junctions or stations, this is clearly impracticable without special methods of working. In the case of engineering works on a double track section where one line is out of use and only one line is available for traffic in both directions, single line working is instituted. This is described in more detail later in this chapter.

In other instances, perhaps following a mishap or failure it may be necessary for a wrong direction movement to be made through or into a block section on a mechanically-signalled line or a section controlled or supervised remotely on a track circuit block line. At one time written train orders were issued to cover such moves but with modern signalling where the signalbox might be many miles away from the location it is not practicable for written instructions to be passed between signalmen and train crews. Since 1972 rules for wrong direction movements have been standardised and generally require the controlling signalman's personal instruction to the driver, given over the telephone if necessary, to make the move. In the case of a train failure where assistance might have to be obtained from a signalbox or other point in advance the assisting locomotive would have to travel in the wrong direction towards the failure after the signalman has been given an assurance that the failed train will not move. If more than one signalbox is involved the signalmen must reach a clear understanding on what is to be done and the driver of the assisting locomotive, which must travel slowly during such moves, must also be given clear instructions on the limits of the wrong direction move. He must have the signalman's personal authority for running over controlled points and must himself make sure that catch points or spring points are properly secured for safe passage before passing through them. If the wrong direction move passes over a level crossing including an automatic half-barrier crossing the locomotive must stop short of the crossing before proceeding to ensure that nobody is taken unaware. As the assisting locomotive nears the failed train it will set off the protecting detonators 300yd away after which the assisting locomotive will be conducted to the train.

On other occasions the assisting locomotive will come from the rear and will be sent into the section under instruction, exploding the protecting detonators behind the failed train. Although it might propel the failure forward it might be more convenient to draw the train back to a previous station, and again the wrong direction move is made under the personal instruction of the signalman to the driver of the assisting locomotive, the detailed procedure being agreed beforehand.

The only occasion when a driver need not obtain the signalman's permission for a wrong direction move is when a train has become divided, both parts have stopped reasonably near each other and are capable of being recoupled, and the front part can set back to recouple without passing over any points or automatic half-barrier level crossings. Even then the controlling signalman must be kept advised of what is being done.

Assisting Engine or Train

In normal working under the absolute block system there can only be one train in a block section on one line at a time. But if a train fails in the section, a second train or engine must be allowed into the section occupied by the failed train to give assistance. Using the previous example of the Ditton-Parkhurst section, if the assisting train or engine is to enter the section in the right direction, that is behind the failed train, the Ditton signalman must first agree with the signalman at Parkhurst by telephone the course of action to be taken. The assisting engine or train is stopped at Ditton signalbox where the signalman explains the circumstances to the driver. The signalman then allows the engine or train to proceed, keeping a look out for the guard walking back (in fog it must wait for the guard). The starting or advanced starting signal is maintained at danger and the Ditton signalman sends the train entering section bell signal to Parkhurst. The assisting engine or train is not offered or accepted in the usual way. If the failed train is propelled right through the section the train out of section signal is sent from Parkhurst to Ditton when the train *and* assisting engine arrives. If the failed train is drawn back to Ditton, clear of the section, the block indicator is afterwards maintained at train on line. The first train to pass through the section in the right direction after the failure must be stopped at Ditton, the driver told to pass the starting or advanced starting signal at danger and proceed cautiously through the section. When this train arrives at Parkhurst the signalman there sends the train out of section signal for it to Ditton, after which normal working may be resumed.

An engine may be sent into the block section without being offered and accepted in the normal way for the purpose of examining the line, perhaps to see if a line is obstructed if there was any previous doubt, or to locate a train which may have failed or suffered a mishap. Before the engine is allowed to leave, the signalmen at each end of the section must agree on the action over the telephone. The train entering section bell signal is sent and the block indicator placed straight to train on line. Here again the engine must pass the starting or advanced starting signal at danger.

On track circuit block lines locomotives or trains used to give assistance to a failed train are instructed by telephone what is required and if one signalbox only is concerned there is of course no exchange of bell signals or operation of block instruments. Where two power signalboxes are involved near the boundary of control areas the two signalmen must agree the course of action.

Obstruction—Danger

If a signalman becomes aware of an obstruction fouling a running line he must immediately send the obstruction danger bell signal (6 beats) to the boxes in the rear and place the block indicator at train on line and his signals at danger for the line or lines obstructed. This bell signal is not preceded by the call attention signal, and may be sent whether or not a train has been accepted, or is actually in the section. This signal would be used to cover any type of obstruction as well as a mishap to a train. The signalman may, for example, be advised that a platform barrow has fallen on the line, or perhaps a car out of control has broken through a fence, run down an embankment and stopped on the line, or the permanent way ganger may telephone to report a broken rail. Having sent the signal, the signalman must take steps to stop any train that may be approaching on any of the affected lines. He should then telephone the signalman at the box to which he sent the obstruction danger signal to explain the reason for giving it.

The signalman receiving the signal must immediately place or maintain his signals at danger and place three detonators 20yd apart on the running lines to prevent any train entering the obstructed section. Having satisfied himself that sufficient protection has been afforded, the signalman receiving the signal must acknowledge it. If he succeeds in stopping a train which had previously been accepted into the now obstructed section, he sends the cancelling signal (3-5). The signalman at the box ahead must acknowledge this signal but must maintain the block instrument at train on line until the obstruction is cleared and the obstruction removed signal can be sent. The obstruction removed signal is the same as the train out of section signal (2-1).

If the signalman receiving the obstruction danger signal is unable to prevent a train which has already been accepted from entering the obstructed section, the obstruction danger signal is not acknowledged but the train running away in right direction signal (4-5-5) sent instead. The signalman receiving this latter signal, who of course sent the original obstruction danger signal, must now take steps to have the approaching train stopped short of the obstruction.

Stop and Examine Train

It is part of a signalman's duty in mechanical signalboxes to watch every train passing his box, and to satisfy himself that the train is complete and running properly. If a door is not properly closed, or if there are signs of smoke from a hot axle-box, or should he spot any other defect on the train, he must take steps to stop the train and, if necessary, trains running on the opposite or adjacent lines. If it is too late to stop the train at his own signals he sends the stop and examine bell signal (7 beats) to the signalbox ahead followed by a telephone message to tell the signalman there what is amiss. On receiving the bell signal the signalman there will restore his signals for the train to danger or caution and bring the train to a stand so that the defect may be examined and, if possible, put right. Where the block sections are short and the signalman receiving the stop and examine signal cannot stop the train he sends on the 7-beat bell signal to the next box ahead. Both the signalman sending and the signalman receiving the stop and examine signal must also stop trains travelling in the opposite direction until it can be established that the opposite line is not obstructed. On track circuit block lines hot axlebox detectors are located at strategic points linked to signalbox warning equipment since in centralised power signalboxes signalmen cannot see the trains they are dealing with.

Train Passed Without Tail-Lamp

All trains on running lines carry tail lamps, attached to the rear of the last vehicle in the train. After dark, or in daylight if the train passes through certain specified tunnels, or during fog or falling snow, this lamp is lit and shows a red light to the rear. The presence of the tail lamp on the rear of a train indicates to the signalman that the train is complete. All but fully-braked freight trains also carry side lamps on the last vehicle. If a train passes without a tail lamp or at night, if the tail light cannot be seen, the signalman must assume that the train is not complete. He therefore sends the train passed without tail lamp bell signal (9) to the box ahead for the train to be stopped there. The train passed without tail lamp (4-5) signal is also sent to the signalbox in rear to advise the signalman there of the position. The signalman who originated the train passed without tail lamp signal must in turn stop trains travelling in the opposite direction but may let them proceed after advising the driver of the situation. If the train is a passenger, parcels or class 4 or 6 freight train all of which are automatically braked throughout, it is possible that the lack of a tail lamp is due to nothing more serious than the tail lamp having fallen off the bracket, or, at night, the flame having blown out. The guard of the train can soon confirm if the train is complete from his journal on which the vehicles in the train are listed. If it is, the tail lamp is re-lit or replaced and the train out of section bell signal given. If the train is found to be incomplete the signalman must take steps to stop the rear part and later to clear it from the section. If a freight train passes without tail or side lamps the signalman must immediately assume that it has become uncoupled and divided into two or more sections and act accordingly. On a rising gradient, for example, the rear part may be running away in the wrong direction. (See page 105).

Train Divided

If both portions of a divided train enter or are likely to run into the section ahead, the signalman sends the train divided bell signal (5-5) to the signalbox ahead, and also takes action to stop all trains on adjoining lines until the emergency has passed. The signalman receiving the signal should stop any train travelling in the opposite direction. He must also decide on his course of action regarding the divided train, which will depend on the location, gradient, and the position of other trains. Where he considers that the stopping of the first portion would risk a collision with the second portion, and he has obtained permission for the train to proceed, or if he has not and considers that sufficient time has elapsed since the passage of the previous train, and certain other conditions are fulfilled, he may authorise the driver to continue into the section ahead by slowly, but conspicuously, waving a green hand signal from side to side. The driver will understand from this that his train is divided, and that he must proceed cautiously into the section ahead, which may be occupied, in order to avoid or reduce the force of a collision between front and rear portions.

If a train becomes divided in starting, leaving the second portion stationary, or if a train is divided in running but the second portion does not enter the section ahead the signalman sends the stop and examine train signal (7) to the box ahead, and not the train divided signal.

In track circuit block areas a divided train will show up by occupying more than one track circuit section. In such cases the signalman may have more flexibility in dealing with the train because of the larger area under his supervision. He might for example, have more chance to keep the line clear for a runaway portion until it can be stopped.

Train Running Away

Runaway trains are, fortunately, rare but nevertheless signalmen must know how to deal with them. They may arise perhaps as a result of a freight train breaking into two, which we mentioned in the last section, or from a number of other causes. If the train or vehicles run without authority along the proper line in the right direction, the signalman sends the train running away in right direction bell signal (4-5-5) to the signalbox ahead and must prevent any further trains from entering the section until the line is again clear.

The signalman receiving the signal must peg the block indicator for the line concerned at train on line and place all his signals at danger, put detonators on the line concerned and take steps to divert the runaway train from the main line. Should a train legitimately be in the section ahead of the runaway, the front train is allowed to pass; the signals must then be placed at danger behind the train, detonators put on the rails, and other steps taken to stop the runaway. If the runaway train emerges intact from the block section complete with tail lamp the train out of section signal is sent to the box in the rear. If, however, a train is in a block section ahead of the runaway, the train out of section signal is not sent until both trains have emerged from the section complete. In either case, the signalman at the rear box may then offer another train in the normal way, but when it has been accepted, he must stop the train and instruct the driver to proceed cautiously through the section.

A similar course of action is taken by a signalman should a train or vehicles escape in the wrong direction. This however is more serious for the runaway train is travelling against the normal flow of traffic. Bell signal 2-5-5 is used and it is sent to the signalbox towards which the runaway train is travelling. The signalman receiving the bell signal must immediately take action to prevent any train proceeding into the section occupied by the runaway, and should, if possible, attempt to turn the runaway into a siding or across to the right line. Should he succeed in turning the train to the right line, but fail to stop it, the train running away in right direction signal (4-5-5) must then be sent to the next signalbox towards which the train is running. If it is established that the runaway train has stopped in the block section, it can be removed by an assisting engine either by being propelled forward or drawn back.

Failure of Block Instruments

The correct working of the absolute block system is dependent on the proper functioning of the block instruments and bells. Should there be a partial or complete failure of instruments and bells, trains are not allowed to enter the block section until the driver and guard of each train have been informed of the situation. Where the bells and block instruments have failed but the telephone is still in operation, trains may be offered and accepted verbally on the telephone by carefully phrased messages; where only the bells have failed, and the block instruments are still functioning, these must be used in conjunction with the telephone messages.

When a complete failure occurs and telephone communication cannot be established, the block system cannot be maintained and signalmen must revert to time-interval working—the system used in the early days of railways before the adoption of the block system. But there are additional safeguards, for trains are not allowed into the section unchecked. When the driver is advised of the failure he is instructed to proceed cautiously so that he may stop his train short of the one in front on sight. A second train must not be allowed to enter the section until the time normally taken by a train to pass through the section, allowing for stops, has elapsed; in any case the time interval must not be less than six minutes and if there is a tunnel in the affected section a second train must not be allowed to proceed for ten minutes, or until the signalman has satisfied himself that the tunnel is clear.

During time-interval working, trains must be brought inside the protection of the home signal as quickly as possible after arrival. If a train requires to stop outside the protection of a home signal to shunt, before so doing, a handsignal-man must first go back to protect the train. When the failure has been rectified, and the instruments are again in working order, the next train to run through the section must be stopped at the signalbox controlling entry to the section, and the driver given a ticket addressed to the signalman at the box ahead to the effect that the train carrying the ticket will be the last train to be cautioned through the section and that normal working may be recommenced. The signalman receiving the ticket sends the train out of section signal when the train arrives, after which normal working is resumed.

H

Single Line Working

It has become the custom for British Railways to carry out extensive engineering works in connection with the modernisation programme, or normal track or bridge renewals, at week-ends. Sometimes the engineers take possession of a complete route and trains are diverted over alternative lines. In other cases the engineers leave one track free for traffic but it has to carry trains in both directions. In these circumstances, or at any time because of an obstruction when the traffic of a double line has to be worked over the remaining single line, a pilotman must be appointed. The pilotman acts instead of the staff or token used on a normal single line. In fact if a single line staff or token is lost or damaged working by pilotman must be introduced in a similar manner.

Single line working past the obstruction is normally confined to the shortest length of line possible, usually from one signalbox to the next, unless the crossover at one box is itself affected by the engineering works, when the single line working operates through two block sections. The person appointed to act as pilotman must wear round his left arm a red armlet, carrying the word pilotman in white letters. No train may enter the single line section without the pilotman, unless two or more successive trains are to pass through the section in the same direction in which case the pilotman must personally order each train except the last to proceed, and ride on the engine of the last train himself. This method of working is akin to the staff and ticket system in which a pilotman acts instead of the staff and his verbal instruction instead of the written ticket. In some cases an engine may be specially provided to enable the pilotman to travel from one end of the section to the other and in this case the engine is coupled ahead of the train engine.

Before single line working can be put into operation it must be officially arranged by a responsible officer such as a station manager or district inspector. To do this he completes special single line working forms and addresses them to the person to act as pilotman, to the signalmen and station managers at both ends of the section of line involved and the signalmen or station managers at any intermediate signalboxes and stations on the line involved which are open while single line working is in operation. All the forms must also be signed by the pilotman and he in turn must obtain the signatures of all the people receiving forms on his own copy. Until the pilotman has delivered the forms and obtained the signatures of the staff concerned at *both* ends of the section, and all level-crossing keepers, gangers, and others at work on the line have been verbally informed by the pilotman that single-line working is to be put into operation,

FIG 46   Single line working past an obstruction.

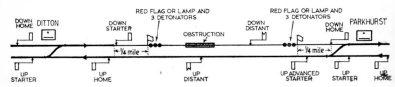

no train must be allowed to travel in the wrong direction over the line to be used as the single line. Thus, the station manager at the station ahead of the obstruction will usually make the arrangements for single line working because the pilotman can, in this case, travel by train in the right direction over the line to be used as the single line when delivering the single line working forms.

The line which has been obstructed or otherwise closed to traffic is protected at each end by three detonators, placed 20yd apart, and a red flag or lamp about ¼ mile ahead of the crossover used by trains to reach the single line, and the same distance to the rear of the crossover where trains leave the single line. The person arranging single line working must ensure that catch or trap points and all unworked points which become facing points are clipped and padlocked. In addition points not equipped with facing point locks which become facing points in one direction must also be clipped.

Block working is maintained if possible—down trains being signalled on the down line instruments and up trains on the up instruments, although all trains run on only one line. If the block instrument for the obstructed line is showing train on line the pilotman instructs the signalman concerned to release the indicator so that block working can continue. Where block instruments are controlled by track circuits, it may not be possible to maintain block working. In such cases, however, the signal engineers' staff may be authorised to disconnect these controls to allow block working to be maintained.

In track circuit block areas where the single line working area may be many miles from the controlling signalbox it may be necessary to have a signalman's agent at the site working the crossover and signals from a ground frame under the direction of the signalman in the powerbox, or alternatively an acting signalman may be appointed to have full local control with telephone communication to his opposite number at the other end of the single line section.

If block working cannot be used, train messages may be sent on the telephone as in the case of a failure. If telephones are not available time interval working must be adopted and in this case the pilotman must accompany every train. Certain signals, particularly those controlling entry to the single line section, are maintained at danger and drivers are instructed to pass them by the pilotman when authorised by the signalman. When double line working can be resumed, the pilotman withdraws the single line working forms.

To speed trains during single line working the WR is installing signalled reversible working and facing crossovers controlled from its power boxes between Didcot and Bristol. On other double track routes with modern signalling, facing crossovers are provided but not reversible signalling.

Fog

Fog, and in winter, a severe blizzard, are probably the railwaymen's greatest enemies. Visibility is reduced, sometimes to no more than a few feet. Semaphore signals become difficult to locate from a moving train and therefore certain signals are provided with a fogsignalman. His job is to repeat the indication of the signal to the driver by means of detonators and flag or lamp signals.

The explosion of a detonator is an additional warning of a signal at danger or caution. In the case of stop and distant arms mounted on the same post, the detonator is removed only when both arms are clear. On busy lines it would be dangerous for the fogsignalman himself to place and remove detonators from the running rails every time a particular signal indication is changed. At many signals, therefore, a fogman's hut is provided. This is equipped with small signal arms which repeat for the fogsignalman's benefit the indication of the signal or signals under supervision. The hut is also equipped with a small lever frame connected via rodding to detonator placing machines, which, like trip arms, are mounted on the sleeper ends beside the running rails.

Normally semaphore stop signals and colour-light signals are not provided with fogsignalmen during fog or falling snow, since every semaphore stop signal is protected by a distant, and colour lights are regarded as being sufficiently powerful to penetrate fog. However, semaphore outer-homes protecting junctions and intermediate block home signals may have fogsignalmen, and at colour-light signals where the overlap to a conflicting junction is short, automatic detonator placers are sometimes provided.

Every signalbox has its own specified fog point which may be a signal post, lamp post or building visible from the box, generally 200yd away which, when obscured by fog or a snowstorm, is an indication that fogsignalmen, who are generally permanent way men, should be called out. Between the time the fogsignalmen are called out, and the time they arrive at their posts, signalmen must institute double block working as an interim safety measure. In double block working, a signalman may not accept a train from the box in the rear until he has received train out of section for the previous train from the box in advance. Using our previous example, Parkhurst cannot accept a train from Ditton unless he has received train out of section for the previous train from Cookfield. In some instances where sections are short a signalman may not accept a train from the rear until it has been accepted by the box ahead. In either case this has the effect of introducing two block sections between trains.

The added restrictions and precautions employed in signalling trains in fog have the effect of increasing the distance between trains and thus reducing the capacity of the line. Thus on lines carrying heavy traffic a special fog service timetable is introduced in which fewer trains are scheduled.

On track circuit block lines colour-light signals can usually penetrate fog and with aws protection drivers can sight signals far more easily than semaphores; thus train services do not normally need to be reduced in fog.

9—Other Signalling Systems
(See diagrams on pages 54, 55 and 56)

Although methods of working and types of signal have been evolved and standardised over many years, a number of signalling experiments have been made on British railways from time to time. Most were on a small scale, some were successful but for various reasons were not adopted, others were quietly forgotten.

Mirfield Speed Signalling

One experiment which survived, although not extended or developed in Britain, was the speed signalling system introduced by the LMS in 1932 over the 2¾ miles between Heaton Lodge Junction and Thornhill LNW Junction at Mirfield, on the lines from Manchester and Huddersfield to Leeds and Wakefield. The standard form of signalling adopted at junctions on British railways was, and still is, by a route indication shown, in semaphore areas, by the clearance of a specific signal arm, or in low speed areas by a route indicator. In colour-light practice, too, drivers receive a definite indication of the route they are to take by the angle of the white-light junction indicator denoting 1st, 2nd or 3rd line to the left or right as the case may be and they regulate the train speed accordingly. But in America, Germany and elsewhere, junction signals display an indication denoting the speed at which a train should run and not the route it is to take.

In the LMS scheme, multiple-aspect searchlight-type colour-light signals were used, but block working and all the existing signal boxes were retained. At junction signals, the lights for diverging routes were placed vertically under the main aspect instead of side-by-side as in current route signalling practice. Thus, the top light (or lights) indicated the highest speed route and the lower light (or lights) the medium speed route—whether to right or left is not indicated. Beneath this group of lights, lower down the post, was a red marker light to indicate that the signal was in a multiple-aspect area; colour-light signals leading to semaphore signals were not provided with a marker light.

In the Mirfield signalling a fifth aspect was adopted in addition to the standard multiple-aspect indications—yellow over green—attention, pass second signal at restricted speed. To obtain the various permutations of signal aspects, junction signals required four lights, the top for the high speed route, the second for the additional light in the two-light indications for either high or medium speed routes, the third for the medium speed route, and finally the marker light.

The marker light also served as an additional danger signal should the main light fail. The red marker remained alight at all times except on non-junction signals displaying a green aspect or where the marker itself changed to a small yellow indication for shunting purposes. The diagrams (page 54) show the indications, from which it will be seen that a junction signal at danger displayed **from** top to bottom: red, out, red, red; the indication pass second signal at restricted speed on high speed route was yellow, green, red, red; and line clear for diverging route red, out, green red. Not all signals in the Mirfield scheme were of the speed type for where the speed over the diverging route varied by less than 20mph from the main route, route-type multiple-signals bracketed side-by-side from the same post were provided, and the marker light was retained where needed.

Although this system sought to overcome many of the anomalies which then existed and, to a certain extent, still exist in semaphore or combined semaphore/colour-light practice, standard three- and four-aspect signalling of the route type with its simple display has become established throughout British Railways where colour-light signals have been adopted. Standard colour-light signals replaced the Mirfield speed signalling installation in the early 1970s. But Mirfield pointed the way and as train speeds increase more positive advanced signalling indications are now thought to be necessary at junctions. The introduction of 125mph trains on the WR in 1976 showed the need for junction distant signals, in the form of flashing aspects. See page 124.

Camden-Watford LMR

Following the Mirfield scheme the LMS installed a related but simpler signalling
system when the suburban electric line from Camden (Euston and Broad Street)
to Watford Junction (known as the New line) and the LMS controlled part of
the District Line from Bromley to Upminster were equipped with colour-light
signals and full track circuiting during 1932-3. The Upminster line has since
been taken over by London Transport and resignalled to LT standards but
the Watford line signalling retains a number of interesting features and is now
the sole example of its type. Signals are of the searchlight pattern and are
basically of two types—stop signals, normally showing red or green, and repeater
signals (in effect distant signals) which show red, yellow, and green. Both stop
and repeater signals have red lower marker lights, except where a colour-light
signal leads to a semaphore area (on connecting lines). The marker light on stop
signals is vertically below the main light, and on the repeater signals below the
main light, but bracketed out about 10in to the left of the post. The marker
light is illuminated only when the main aspect is at danger or in the event of a
lamp failure in the main aspect. In normal working, a train cannot approach a
repeater signal showing red. There are also some three-aspect stop signals which
show red, yellow and green where successive stop signals are required to protect
junctions, and there are one or two other unique signals at junctions. All stop
signals are equipped with electrically-operated train-stop trip apparatus. Except
at junctions and certain stations, signals are automatic but some signalboxes can
be closed during part of the day and the signals left to function automatically;
even where boxes remain open, certain levers can be left in reverse for the signals
concerned to work automatically. On most of the line, signals are alternately
stop and repeaters. As a train proceeds it will place each signal to danger as it
passes. When it clears the overlap track circuit beyond a stop signal, the previous
repeater changes from red to yellow and the previous stop signal from red to
green. In some cases the overlap track circuit extends nearly to the next repeater
ahead so that when that signal goes to danger, for a few seconds there may be
four signals at danger behind the train, two stop signals and two repeaters, but
one stop and one repeater soon change to green and yellow respectively. Thus,
there is at least one stop signal and a train-stop at danger between every train.
Unlike the Mirfield installation, junction stop signals are not of a speed type but
have separate bracketed signals to indicate a divergence. The few junction
distants on the Watford line are also stop signals. The signals concerned show
four aspects—red, yellow, double yellow and green, plus the marker light in
the danger position. Two additional yellow lights are provided, one on each
side of the main lights but are illuminated only when required to give the
junction indications. The diagrams on page 55 show the aspects. The primary
feature is that the main centre lights provide the signal aspects regardless of
which route ahead is set. When the junction ahead is set for the left-hand route,
the *right*-hand side light is illuminated so that the main aspect is the left-hand
of the pair, denoting route set for left-hand divergence. Similarly, when the
route is set for the right-hand divergence, the *left*-hand side light is illuminated
so that the main aspect is to the right.

The most unusual feature of the Watford line signalling is the automatic

Above left: A junction signal on the experimental LMS Mirfield speed signalling system.

[*K. Field*

Above: A stop and splitting distant signal on the LMS Camden-Watford electric line.

[*G. M. Kichenside*

Above right: A repeater signal on the Camden-Watford line.

[*British Railways*

Left: A London Transport type floodlit disc shunting signal with a theatre-type route indicator.

[*London Transport*

Right: London Transport two-aspect colour-light stop signal with a disc distant signal to give locomotive-hauled freight trains a greater braking distance than that needed for LT electric trains.

calling-on arrangement. If a train is stopped at an automatic stop signal at danger, but the overlap track circuit of that signal is clear a 70-80sec time release operates, the trip arm drops, the red marker light changes to a miniature yellow light, and the train may proceed at caution, but the driver must be ready to stop short of any obstruction. In this way a train may approach a repeater signal showing red. The red repeater is an added protection behind a train at a stop signal ahead. If a train is then stopped at a red repeater, after a wait of one minute it may proceed cautiously past the signal at danger, again with the driver ready to stop short of any obstruction. Repeater signals have no trip apparatus nor does the marker light change. These calling-on arrangements apply only at automatic signals or at controlled signals when working automatically. It has the advantage of quickly overcoming local signal failures but in the event of a prolonged hold up in the past, when the line had a more intensive service than now, it sometimes produced the spectacle of several trains together buffer to buffer one behind the other!

London Transport (*See diagrams on page 56*)

Signalling on the London Underground railways has more-or-less followed main line practice but has been adapted to suit the different conditions peculiar to an urban electrified rapid transit system. With the exception of a few freight trains operated by British Railways over certain LT surface lines, all London Transport trains consist of electric multiple-units. Thus all trains on a line have the same rapid acceleration and braking characteristics and the signalling is designed to make the best use of these features. In places, trains may follow one another at no more than 1min intervals and braking distances and overlaps beyond stop signals are short. At the approaches to stations and conflicting junctions, closely-spaced signals allow a train to close up towards the one in front or to draw right up to a junction after its speed has been reduced to within pre-determined limits.

All London Transport lines are fully track-circuited and colour-light signals are installed almost throughout the system. Stop signals, all of which are fitted with train-stop trip apparatus, show red or green; repeater signals show yellow or green. Sometimes a repeater signal is mounted on the same post underneath the previous stop signal rather like a British Railways semaphore stop and distant signal. In this case these signals may appear to be capable of showing four aspects but in fact only display three—red, green over yellow, double green. Quite often, particularly in tunnel sections where the driver's view of the line ahead is good, repeaters may not be provided and trains may have to stop on sight at a danger signal. At the other extreme, on parts of the Metropolitan line and formerly parts of the Central line, where British Railways freight trains operated over LT tracks, the normal LT repeater signals would not provide sufficient braking distance to the next stop signal for these trains and floodlit disc distant signals have been provided about 1000yd to the rear of the first stop signal.

Approaching a station the usual signals provided are: a repeater for the group of home signals protecting the platform, the home signals themselves, usually three, and under the last a repeater for the platform starting signal; finally the starting signal itself. One or two repeaters of the starting signal are usually

Above: The push-button panel at Amersham signal cabin on London Transport's Metropolitan line.

[*London Transport*

Right: A London Transport programme machine used in automatic junction control, showing the sensitive feelers which detect and transmit electrical impulses through perforations in the programme roll.

[*London Transport*

Below: London Transport's Coburg Street control room which supervises complete operation on the Northern and Victoria lines.

[*London Transport*

provided along the platform or by the tunnel entrance, for the guidance of station staff. Additional stop (and sometimes repeater) signals are provided between stations to permit close headways. At some stations the group of home signals is provided with a speed control device which measures the speed of an approaching train. If a train is standing in a station a following train will be checked at the first home of the group and when its speed has been reduced to within certain limits the signal will clear and allow the train forward towards the second home signal. When the first train proceeds, and clears the rear part of the platform, the second of the home signals clears for the following train. Finally as the first train passes beyond the overlap of the starting signal the last of the home signals clears and admits the train to the platform.

At facing junctions, as on British Railways, approach control may be used to ensure that a train's speed has been reduced before the signal clears. Except at junctions or stations where crossing movements are made, signalling is automatic and controlled by the trains themselves. Power operation was adopted at an early date by the Underground railways and is now used almost exclusively by London Transport. Remote control of junctions and stations is adopted where possible and the Stanmore branch was operated from its opening by a form of centralised traffic control (ctc) from Wembley Park cabin. Many signal cabins are provided with miniature-lever frames, some working on the one lever —one function principle, others on the route-setting principle. London Transport's last new local signal cabins commissioned in the early 1960s were equipped with route-setting push-button panels, although with the buttons as a group and not mounted geographically on the track diagram. The operation of one push-button sets up a complete route; the button is self-restoring and needs no further action by the signalman after the move is completed. In some cases route pre-selection is possible and the signalman can operate a button to set a second conflicting route while the first is still set up. The second route is held in store and is set up automatically only when the route becomes free after the first move is completed.

During the last decade London Transport has been developing automatic control of junctions to ease the work of signalmen and in the long term to dispense with local signalmen altogether in the quest for the fully automated railway. At simple facing junctions the automatic train describers can be used to control the junction points; at trailing junctions, signals can be arranged to pass trains on a first come-first served basis with, of course, the usual safety precautions so that if two trains should arrive together one would be given precedence over the other.

One of the most ingenious developments in junction or station control is the programme machine which London Transport has installed in recent years in many places to work points automatically. The programme machine carries a plastic roll about 8ft long and 8in wide, on which is typed the day's train service showing the time, number and destination of each train. Alongside each entry is a series of punched holes forming a code. Feeler arms on the programme machine press against the roll and as the coded holes come into position, contacts on the feeler arms read the code and initiate the setting-up of the appropriate route for the train. As each train proceeds, the programme machine roll is automatically stepped to the next entry. The programme machine normally works in conjunction with a time machine and also checks with the train describer that the correct train is approaching so that it will only set the route if all is in order and that the time is right for it to do so. If a train is late by more than a pre-set time, the machine may sound an alarm in the supervision room or, if trains arrive at a converging junction out of order the machine may automatically step forward to deal with the train that has arrived first, storing the route details in its memory until the missing train arrives. The programme machines themselves do not directly operate signals and points. This is still done by LT's interlocking machines as in installations controlled by miniature levers or push buttons. The programme machines simply replace the signalman and his action of pulling a lever or pressing a button. The programme machine has brought London Transport to the position where complete lines can be controlled by automation, and supervised by one central control room.

Programme machines control junctions and station timing signals throughout the Victoria and Northern Lines and on several other sections of London Transport's railway network. The whole of the Victoria and Northern Lines are supervised from a control centre at Coburg Street near Euston staffed by a signal regulator and traffic controller for each line. In this room track diagrams showing all tracks of both lines display the position of every train, the indications of selected signals, the train descriptions giving the identity of each train as it approaches a programme machine interlocking area, and by coloured lights how each programme machine is working. Normally programme machines work in conjunction with the train describer in which case a steady green light is displayed on the control panel. If the signal regulator switches the programme machine at a junction to work on a first come, first served, basis the fect is denoted on the control panel by a yellow light. If train working gets well out of timetable order it might be necessary for the signal regulator to set routes manually by push-buttons in his control desk to over-ride the machine shown by a red light against the programme machine concerned on the diagram. Sometimes it might only be necessary for the signal regulator to step the programme machine forward to the next entry because a train is cancelled in which case the basic automatic operation is not disturbed.

During 1973 London Transport started experiments with a small on-line computer to replace programme machines at Watford (Metropolitan Line) with supervision from Rickmansworth. Only the programme machine functions have been taken over by the computer, all other equipment including the interlocking machine remaining as before. LT is also planning computer supervision of the Victoria and Northern Line programme machines in the Coburg Street control centre as another trial to take some of the routine and programme machine management tasks off the traffic controller and signal regulator, particularly during service disruptions. The computer would give more facilities for automatic recording and would be capable of giving the controller information to m ke best use of crew and train availability. During 1974 the Watford computer installation was linked for extended trials to a coloured visual display unit (vdu) in Rickmansworth signal cabin. The vdu provides a simpler, clearer picture, and occupies less space than a conventional track diagram. The unit consists of a 22in colour tv monitor screen with eight selector switches to enable the signalman to vary the information displayed. Unoccupied tracks are

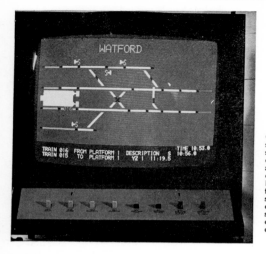

Colour television display unit
showing track occupation and
signal indications linked to
computer-controlled signalling
at Watford LT. The visual
display unit is situated in
Rickmansworth signal cabin
from which the Watford
signalling is supervised. By
operation of the switches the
signalman can add to the
display information required
only occasionally.
[*London Transport*

in blue, occupied tracks in red; normally signals are shown only for trains
occupying tracks.

LT Automatic Train Operation

After experiments in automatic train operation on short sections of existing
lines London Transport introduced the automated railway to Britain with the
opening of the Victoria Line in stages during 1968-9. Victoria Line trains still
have a man at the front, the train operator, but apart from opening and closing
doors and operating the start button at stations his function is supervisory, and
subsequent movement of the train is controlled automatically. Heart of the
Victoria Line signalling system are the two types of coded current signals
carried in the running rails and picked up by induction coils on the front of
each train. The continuous safety signalling codes provide for four situations
based on codes of 420, 270, and 180 impulses per min, or no code at all. The
420 signalling code allows a train to accelerate up to a maximum speed of 50mph
under normal conditions; the 270 code allows a train to run under power up
to a maximum of 25mph; the 180 code allows a train to run up to 25mph
maximum while coasting. If no code is present the train cannot be started, or
if code is lost while travelling the train is brought to an emergency stop.

The second type of code provides driving command spots transmitted to the
train from short 10ft lengths of running rails. High frequency codes are
employed based on 100 cycles per sec (Hz) for each 1mph. Thus a code of
3000Hz will be transmitted to give a speed of 30mph. Command spots are
located in all positions where train speed needs to be regulated, at the approach
to stations, headway points, junctions and speed restrictions. They can be
installed temporarily to control the speed of trains for engineering speed

Station A	15 kc/s (coasting)	20kc/s (brake application)		3·5	3	2·5	2	1 kc/s	Station B		
420	420	420		420	180	120		Station B	420	420	
420	420	420	'ON'	420	270	120	120				420
420	420	420	'ON'	420	270	270	120	120			
420	420	420	'ON'	420	270	270	180	120	120		
420	420	420	'ON'	420	270	270	180	180	180	120	
			'ON'								

IG 47 Diagram showing the safety signalling codes transmitted to trains for automatic -ain operation on London Transport lines so equipped. The 120 code is not detected by -ains and initiates an emergency brake application. Also shown are command spots to switch ff traction motors, and to start service brake applications for signal and station stops.

estrictions. The only exception to the driving command codes is on starting rom a station stop where the accelerating sequence is initiated by the train perator pressing two start buttons. This can be done only with the train eceiving a 420 code after the doors are proved to have closed and the cab side vindow is shut. The latter is a safety precaution to ensure that the train cannot tart with the train operator looking out and possibly striking his head against he tunnel wall. After a signal stop between stations a safety signalling code of 70 impulses is transmitted to the train to switch on the traction motors auto-natically since the 420 code cannot start a train.

Although in the normal way train operation on the Victoria Line is governed •y signalling codes transmitted from the track so that in theory visual signals are ot required, in practice normal lineside signals have been provided at certain ocations, particularly at stations and junctions, to cover a possible failure of he signalling codes. In this case trains are driven manually by the train operator •ut with speed governed to a maximum of 10mph if codes are not being received t all, or 25mph if codes are being received but the train equipment has failed. 'ictoria Line trains are fitted with electro-pneumatic trip apparatus so that if peed exceeds the maximum for the signalling conditions or if codes are lost vhile running the train is automatically brought to an immediate stop.

'yne & Wear Metro

.he new Tyne & Wear Metro system linking the centre of Newcastle with the oastal resorts north of the River Tyne and the industrial towns on both north nd south banks of the river itself, largely utilises former BR tracks which at ne time were electrified and more recently diesel worked. The Metro, electri-ed on the 1500V dc overhead system is a concept new to Great Britain although ne common on mainland Europe. The trains are lighter than conventional rains and effectively are a cross between modern trams and normal trains. .hey are high capacity units, with rapid acceleration and braking; and the 'yne & Wear trains are formed of two articulated car bodies to a single unit, nd up to three units can be coupled together.

The Metro is a full railway since its trains call only at stations and track is n its own right of way. From a signalling point of view, with the rapid braking haracteristics of the trains, braking distances can be short and a simple two-spect colour-light signalling system is provided. Inductive train stops are

used to prevent trains from overrunning stop signals at danger and this equip
ment is also used with timing circuits to verify train speed and for checking
train speed approaching terminal stations. The Tyne & Wear signalling system
draws on modern BR and London Transport practice; control of signals and
points and supervision of the line and its power supplies is from a central con
trol room at South Gosforth, equipped with a one-control switch (OCS) route
setting panel and an illuminated track diagram showing routes set, train pos
itions, lie of points etc, and linked to nine remotely controlled relay inter
lockings. Visual Display units (see page 130) give the controllers displays of
electrical circuit conditions, and train information fed from the computer at the
centre of data transmission and reception from train-mounted transponders.

Private Tourist Railways

The growth of preserved railways during the last 25 years, in which closed
lines of both standard and narrow gauge have been taken over by enthusiast
societies to run as tourist attractions with steam locomotives, has also brought
a reversion to the more basic forms of signalling and train operation. On British
Railways, signalling is gradually becoming far more automated with centralised
control from a few strategically placed signal control centres, often supervising
several hundred miles of line.   The local steam tourist railways, in contrast
often run no more than about five miles or so, and control is very localised
with the aim of preserving the old-time steam railway, semaphore signalling
worked from mechanical signal boxes at individual stations, is a feature of many
of the lines. Thus operation follows very much the practice described for single
lines by staff or token working on page 63, since most lines are of single track
Nearly all the privately-operated tourist railways run under the authority of
what is known as a Light Railway Order, which stems from government
legislation of 1896 and later, which allowed the construction of branch lines
with less stringent requirements in respect of operating facilities than had to
be provided on normal main lines. Signalling is one area which under a Light
Railway Order can be less complex than on a normal line. For example, distant
signals need not be provided, as long as the stop signals can be seen for at least
$\frac{1}{4}$ mile, telephones may be used for the operation of the block system instead
of block instruments, and open ground frames may be used instead of a fully
equipped signalbox. However, the less stringent requirements usually bring
a more restricted form of operation, usually with a low maximum speed of
around 20-40mph, depending on the line and its circumstances.

Many of today's preserved steam tourist railways are former British Railways
standard gauge lines, originally worked under normal arrangements but with
operation now under a Light Railway Order as being the simplest method of
transferring operation of the line to the new company. Having said that a
Light Railway Order allows some relaxation of operating requirements, in fact
since most of the steam tourist railways have holiday peaks, requiring the
operation of more than one train, the signalling requirements on certain lines
are just as stringent as on a BR-worked passenger line. Moreover, the tourist
railways have the problem of varying traffic patterns since early and late in the
holiday season the number of passengers on offer does not require more than the
basic minimum service which may be of one train only. During the peak July

nd August holiday months in contrast, the number of passengers wanting to travel may require several trains to operate an adequate service. Thus, train operation may vary from the basic one engine in steam to an intensive service requiring crossing movements at all the passing loops on a line. This is particularly the case on the narrow gauge lines in Wales and the Lake District where, on the Talyllyn, Festiniog, and Ravenglass & Eskdale lines, as many as three or even four trains may be on the move at one time. Yet, when the line is working with only one train, and a one-engine-in-steam staff could be used, if electric token instruments are employed without switching-out facilities each signalbox must be staffed in order to work the electric tokens for that one train. One alternative with this form can be what are known as no-signalman tokens, where the fireman of a train operates the token instrument for the section ahead without any signalmen being present. The instruments are broadly similar to those described on page 65 but are designed so that when the fireman wants to remove a token he must first operate the instrument to prove that no other token is already out of the two machines at each end of the section and that they are in phase. He can then withdraw a token, the train proceeds through the section and when it reaches the far end of the section the token is put in the instrument there to clear the section, and free the instruments to allow another train to proceed in either direction.

Where passenger trains cross at passing loops on steam tourist railways the Department of Transport inspecting officers normally require a signalbox to be fully manned for such moves. Indeed, since many of the tourist lines operate services which are just as intense as any BR steam-operated commuter line of twenty or more years ago, signalling procedure and operating discipline must be of a high order and although many lines are worked by amateur volunteer railwaymen they must be fully trained and qualified before they are allowed to touch any of the signalling equipment.

Radio Control

One line which carries a very intensive peak train service on a nominal single track line is the Ravenglass & Eskdale running over the seven miles between Ravenglass and Dalegarth. This is a 15in gauge line which in its present form dates broadly from the early 1920s, although it was originally built in the 1870s as a 3ft gauge mineral railway. For many years the line was worked with only one passing loop at Irton Road, on the timetable and train order system which had managed to survive since the line was not within the jurisdiction of the Ministry of Transport. Later when moves were made to formalise railway operation in conformity with the Ministry's requirements it was clear that more positive methods of single line operation would be required. Moreover, since the tourist traffic to the Lake District had increased during the 1960s and early 1970s it was clear that additional passing loops would be required and various methods of operation were considered. Although an electric token system could have been installed, the railway received the approval of the Ministry of Transport's inspecting officers for a trial installation of radio control between a central control office and all motive power units. Each locomotive on the line is equipped with radio transmitter and receiver by which the driver can talk to the controller situated in the signalbox at Raven-

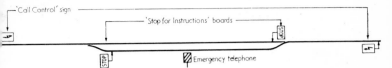

FIG 48 Layout at a typical Ravenglass & Eskdale Railway crossing loop showing signs instructing drivers to call the controller.

Mass. The signalbox lever frame here is used only for controlling points and signals in Ravenglass Station, but the controller is in charge for operating the block system and passing moves at crossing stations on the whole line. The radio frequencies are arranged so that the controller can talk to and be heard by all drivers at the same time, but each driver in talking to control can only be heard by the controller. So that there is no possibility of confusion each locomotive has a call sign depending on the train number that it is working at the time. The call sign for the whole system uses the code word 'Rander' based on the initials of the railway—R and ER. The traffic controller has a train graph in front of him based on the normal time/distance arrangement. All the possible train paths are lightly printed on the sheet. The basis of the system is that the controller instructs a train to proceed from point A to point B and at the same time the controller draws a red line horizontally along the graph from point A to point B to indicate to himself that the section is occupied. The train then proceeds and when the driver reports that he is clear of that single line section, inside the passing loop at point B, the controller draws a green line on the graph corresponding to the path taken by the train, and the section is then free for the controller to authorise either another train to proceed in the same direction or for a train in the opposite direction, and again he draws a

FIG 49 Portion of a control graph representing a possible R&ER service; the arrows on the graph depict the red lines on the controller's graph to show line occupied. The thick lines show the train's path and are drawn in green after arrival at a loop to show the rear section is clear.

Left: R&ER motive power is equipped with radio transmitter/receivers to allow drivers to talk to the controller.   [R&ER

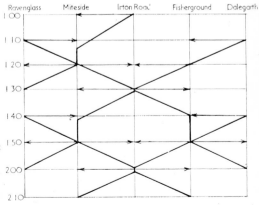

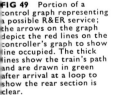

J

red line to indicate that the section is again blocked by an authorised move.
Thus the train graph appears as a pattern of alternate red and green lines for
each section.

Apart from trains about to leave Ravenglass, where the driver is given a
written train order by the controller as his authority to proceed from Ravenglass
to Miteside, the drivers mark on the train order arrows when they are given
further instructions to proceed. Drivers are required to call up the controller by
radio, when approaching a passing loop both to report their position and to
enquire for instructions as to their moves in the next passing loop. If another
train is approaching the passing loop in the opposite direction and a passing
move is to be made, then the controller will tell both drivers to enter the passing
loops and stop for further instructions, unless the position of the trains is such
that one train can be brought to a stop in the loop and its driver report by radio
that he is clear of the single line and loop points before the second train arrives,
in which case the driver of the second train may be told to proceed through
the loop if there is no need for a stop for station purposes. At all times though,
even with only one train on the line, there is a set procedure to be observed, and
drivers must only be instructed to proceed one section at a time. In the case
of a communication failure of the radio equipment, each station and passing
loop is provided with a telephone link with the control office but in this case
the train must come to a stop in the passing loop for the driver to leave the
locomotive and call up the controller by telephone for instructions. The new

Date 14-9-74		Driver PETER		
Controller Jow		Guard MARTIN		
/		RANDER 16		
Schedule	Xings		Authority	Warnings etc.
1.30		Ravenglass	▓▓▓ ↓	P.W.S 3/4
1.39		Miteside	↓	P.S.W. 3/4-1/2
1.50/50	X / VII	Irton Road	↓	
2.00		Fisherground	↓	
2.10		Dalegarth	↓ ▓▓▓	P.W.S 5 3/4-6

Driver's Comments:

Left margin captions:

*t: Ravenglass control
fice. In front of the
ntroller is the train
aph by which he keeps a
cord of train movement,
d his right hand is on the
icrophone by which he
lls up trains by radio.
[R&ER*

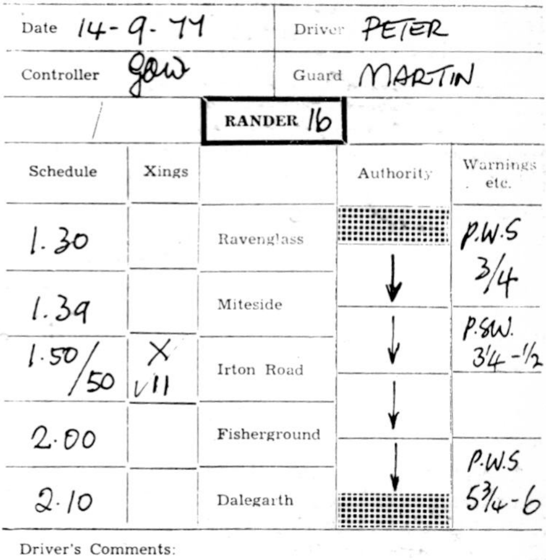

*G 50   R&ER Driver's
ain order made out by
e controller and issued
the driver as an
thority to proceed to the
st crossing station, with
bsequent instructions by
dio.*

stem is being watched with interest by both the railway authority and the
Ministry of Transport, and is the first application of radio controlled block
orking in Britain, although it is used on a number of light and branch rail-
ays in Europe.

10—The Future

n this account we have traced the development of British signalling from
e start of railways to the present-day. It is difficult to foretell future signalling
evelopments, but the future of the conventional railway in high speed form
ems assured at least into the next century, before any other form of guided
nd transport can be fully developed as a competitor. Many lines, including
rmer main lines, have been closed and traffic concentrated on fewer routes.
rviving lines carry heavy traffic and modern signalling is playing a large part.
lock working and semaphore signalling are rapidly giving way to track circuit
ock with colour-light signals and centralised control from power signalboxes
hich now control more than 40 per cent of BR route mileage.

Already, diesel high-speed trains also known as Inter City 125 trains (IC
5.), of 125mph, are in daily service on Western Region lines between London,
ristol and South Wales and the East Coast main line between Kings Cross
d Edinburgh, running under the control of conventional lineside signalling

and aws without any other form of cab signalling. Because of the great
improved braking characteristics of IC 125 trains and their ability to stop fro
125mph in the same distance as a conventional train travelling at 100mph th(
can operate on lines signalled for 100mph running at the higher speed witho
any alteration to signal spacing.

Flashing Yellow aspects

Because of the superior braking of IC 125s it has been necessary to amend t!
standard British four-aspect colour-light signalling indications to include tw
more aspects, a flashing single yellow and a flashing double yellow aspect, ahea
of specified diverging junctions. In standard British colour-light practic
advanced junction indications of lower speed divergences from otherwi
high-speed principal tracks are not normally provided, and the only positi\
indication the driver receives is at the junction signal itself displaying a whit
light route indicator (see pages 29 and 52). Junction signals are normall
approach controlled by the train itself if the route ahead is set for a divergin
track, the form of control varying according to the speed of the junction.

In its basic lowest speed form the junction signal itself is held at danger unt
the train approaches within a given timed distance related to the theoretical spec
of the train correctly slowing down as it approaches the signal; the signal w
clear to a proceed aspect—line conditions ahead being suitable—when the tra\
is at a point by which time speed should have been reduced to that of the turno\
ahead. Thus, the train will have passed the previous colour-light signals showir
caution indications, ie double yellow and then single yellow. In the case (
higher-speed turnouts, of 50mph or more the signal aspects may be less restri(
tive, and the junction signal itself may show a single yellow with a white ligl
junction indicator and the signal preceding it a double yellow, in order t
check the train speed before reaching the junction. A colour-light signal c
plain line displaying double yellow indicates to the driver that he must expect t
find the next signal ahead showing single yellow, and the one beyond that i
red; in four-aspect areas braking distance is provided between the doub!
yellow and the red signal. A problem was seen to arise with IC 125 trair
where a double yellow aspect is used as a caution indication preceding a junctic
signal at single yellow under approach control conditions for a diverging rout
particularly if the junction indicator is not clearly sighted. Because of tl
superior braking of IC 125 trains a driver approaching a double yellow coul
rightly think that it was showing that indication because the second sign
ahead was at danger and he would control his braking in order to stop at th

FIG 51 Signalling sequence at high-speed turnout, with flashing yellow aspects preceding
the junction signal.

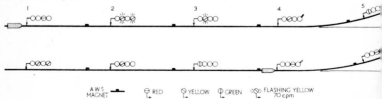

AWS
MAGNET   ◼   ♈ RED   ♀ YELLOW   ♅ GREEN   ⚡ FLASHING YELLOW
                                                      70 cpm

second signal ahead. But if the junction signal is at single yellow with the route set for a lower speed divergence he could in fact approach that signal and the junction points travelling at too high a speed.

Flashing yellow indications have thus been devised to provide a positive warning that the train is signalled to take a diverging route at a junction ahead at a lower speed than the line limit for the straight route. Figure 51 illustrates the use of the flashing yellow indications in a sequence of five four-aspect signals, of which No 4 is the junction signal. When the route is set for a train to run on the normal high-speed through route, and provided the line is clear, the signals will normally show unrestricted green aspects throughout. However, for a train taking the diverging route, calling for a lower speed through the junction points for the divergence, signal No 5 beyond the junction is held at red, even though the signalman may have cleared the route beyond that signal. This means that signal No 4 will show a single yellow with the junction indicator illuminated for the divergence. Signal No 3, however, instead of showing the normal steady double yellow aspect in fact shows a single flashing yellow, while signal No 2 shows a flashing double yellow indication. Signal No 1 at this time can show a green aspect. All the signals are accompanied by aws magnets on the track placed at the normal 200m distance in advance, and all except that for the green signal will give the driver a caution indication When a train approaches the flashing signals the driver will know that the train is signalled to take a diverging route calling for a reduction in speed from the line limit and he will adjust his speed accordingly. He will pass the flashing signals and approach the steady single yellow aspect of the junction signal No 4, which will hold at single yellow until the train has passed its related aws magnet and thus received a caution indication. If the line conditions beyond signal No 5 permit, that signal will then clear from red to green and the junction signal from single yellow to green, and it is entirely up to the driver then to control the train speed to the maximum allowed through the turnout.

Although the flashing yellow sequence was devised primarily with IC 125s in mind, it has been designed to be applicable not only to 100/125mph lines but also on lines with a lower general limit than 100mph. The speeds at which flashing yellows are likely to be used are:

Straight route speed 100mph or over—minimum turnout speed 50mph.

Straight route speed 95mph or less—minimum turnout speed 40mph.

Straight route speed 75 mph or less—minimum turnout speed 30mph.

In all these cases the turnout speed must be more than 10mph below the straight route speed.

This sequence also involves a change in the approach control methods described on page 30 where approach controls are released by a timing relay triggered off as the train occupies the approach or berth track curcuit; in the new sequence using flashing yellows the junction signal itself and the signal beyond the junction will be triggered off, if conditions permit, to a less restrictive aspect without a time release when the train occupies the approach or berth track circuit immediately after passing the aws magnet related to the junction signal. This means that approaching a junction a train taking the diverging route will pass three aws magnets giving a caution indication in the cab.

If for any reason the flashing mechanism fails so that the single yellow No
signal shows a steady aspect, then automatically a more restrictive approach
release of the junction signal will be initiated; in this instance signal 2 will show
a steady double yellow and the junction signal itself will be held at red to ensure
that the driver sees it change to a proceed aspect with the junction indicator
illuminated. If the flashing double yellow aspect fails so that a steady aspect is
displayed, it will in any case be a more restrictive indication and provided that
the single yellow aspect ahead is flashing then the normal clearance can still
apply. In three-aspect signalled areas only one flashing aspect is used, a flashing
single yellow preceding a steady single yellow on the junction signal.

Speed Restrictions and aws

Right from the earliest days of railways engine drivers have been expected to
have expert knowledge of the tracks over which they are working. They must
know the gradients, signalling and places where speed must be restricted
because of physical conditions or points etc. Although speed limits were listed
in various official railway publications issued as an appendix to the timetable
restrictions were rarely marked out on the line and drivers were expected to
control the speed of their trains entirely on their own initiative and knowledge
of the line. Alone of the four group railways the LNER made some attempt
to assist the driver by marking the more important restrictions, particularly on
open line and on high-speed routes at junctions, with white stencil figures
showing the limit at that point mounted on a post alongside the line. British
Railways eventually adopted this system for use throughout the network but
its one defect lay in the fact that the cut-out signs were generally placed at the
start of a restriction so that if a driver had overlooked the need to reduce speed
at that point, by the time he saw the sign it would have been too late anyway,
particularly for a severe restriction on an otherwise high-speed line.

Over the years there have been a number of unexplained high-speed derail-
ments where engine crews have ignored often well publicised restrictions with
heavy loss of life in the resulting derailment. Clearly the railway authorities
regarded them as little more than isolated incidents, for nothing was done in the
way of providing any automated protection to prevent a recurrence until the
1969 high-speed derailment at Morpeth on the East Coast main line, where a
40mph limit exists for a sharp curve on an otherwise high-speed main line.
An overnight sleeping car train approached the restriction at 80mph and the
coaches overturned. With the prospect of even higher line speeds in the
future, the Ministry of Transport recommended the use of aws permanent
magnets giving a caution indication in advance of an illuminated warning board
showing the speed limit in yellow figures on a black background placed at

FIG 52   Lineside indicators and aws permanent magnet arrangement at permanent speed
restriction. There is no indication at the end of the limit.

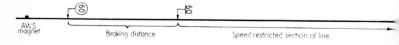

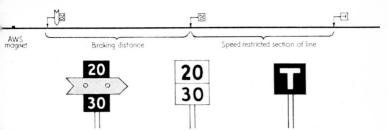

FIG 53 Lineside indicators and portable aws permanent magnet arrangement at temporary speed restrictions. Sometimes trains of coaching stock, not including our-wheelers, can run through the restriction at a higher speed, in which case two speed levels are displayed on the indicators.

braking distance from the restriction. Even then the advance warnings and aws equipment were only to be provided on lines with a general limit of 75mph or over for restrictions to two thirds or less of line speed. They did not apply at junctions since the normal approach control of signalling for diverging routes would provide drivers with a caution indication, though without any advanced indication of the exact speed for the divergence.

Temporary speed restrictions for engineering works or during emergencies, by their variable location and speed, have always been marked by lineside signs as well as appearing in a weekly engineering notice. Three boards are generally

FIG 54 Lineside signs for speed limits and other purposes: **1** Advance warning board (floodlit) for a 60mph permanent speed restriction, **2** Commencement of 60mph permanent speed restriction, but a yellow triangle indicates a variation in the limit for certain classes of train. If the triangle points down the speed variation is lower, if it points up it is higher. **3** 'AWS warning does not apply' indicator, for use with temporary speed restriction magnet in opposite direction on single line. **4** No AWS in operation (at approach to certain major stations). **5** AWS in operation (on leaving those stations). **6** Catch points. **7** Whistle.

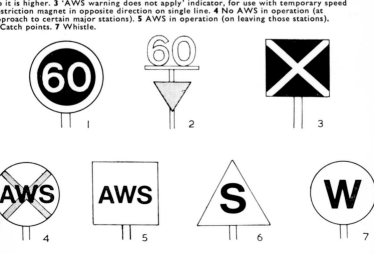

provided: the advanced warning is in the form of a rectangular board with a fishtail cut-out at the lefthand end and an arrow pointing towards the track at the righthand end, and painted yellow, with the speed limit in white figures on black above it; the commencement board, which until a few years ago was a letter C but more recently has been the figures of the speed limit; and finally a board displaying a letter T denoting the end of the restriction. The advance warning board displays two horizontal yellow lights at night and the speed limit figures are illuminated from within, and the commencement and terminating boards also have internal illumination. On some lines the boards are floodlit by electricity if a supply is available or by propane gas where it is not. Oil lamps are still used in these boards, although propane gas lighting is also used. Until 1977 the advance warning board was placed a fixed distance from the commencement board depending on the line speed limit, and on 100mph routes could be as much as 1¼ miles from the commencement of the restriction. Again no attempt was made to provide an automated warning to ensure that the driver could not fail to see the advance warning. The Nuneaton derailment in 1975 occurred when all three lights in the advance warning board had failed and were out so that the board was invisible to the driver of an overnight sleeper train. This fault, combined with poor lighting on the commencement board, led to the train approaching a 20mph restriction at near 80mph and it was badly derailed with several passengers killed. As a result of this accident portable aws permanent magnets giving a caution indication, were adopted from 1977, to be placed about 200 metres before the advanced warning board, on lines where aws is generally installed. Moreover, many of the lineside boards were quite old, and new lighter, high visibility boards were recommended for the future. Independent portable aws magnets accompanying an advanced speed limit warning board will not be provided where the warning board is near a signal which itself has aws, in which case the electro-magnet at the signal which would give the clear indication is disconnected so that the driver still receives a caution indication denoting the presence of the warning board even though the signal may itself be showing clear. On single lines it is not possible to suppress the caution magnet of an aws indication for a temporary speed restriction and trains travelling in the opposite direction will pick up a caution indication which does not apply to them. In this instance a lineside board with a white diagonal cross on a black background tells the driver that he can cancel the aws since it does not apply to him.

Sometimes sections of line may be subject to more than one speed restriction in a short length, in which case the indications on the lineside boards may have to overlap, where for example a more severe limit is provided over a short section within a less restricted section, or where two different restrictions follow consecutively. In some cases a speed restricted section of line might have two speed levels, depending on the type of train. This will be displayed by two sets of figures, one above the other, the top figure showing the lower speed applicable to all trains, except passenger and empty coaching stock trains not including four-wheeled vehicles, and the bottom figure with the higher speed applying to passenger and empty coaching stock trains, provided they do not include four-wheeled vehicles.

A transponder unit fixed between the rails, and now installed generally between Euston and Glasgow for the Advanced Passenger Train. Transponders are packages of electronic equipment, unpowered but brought to life by an inducted signal from a passing train and returning a signal to the train with information about that location.   [British Railways.

Transponders

Chapter 7 describes recent developments on British Railways in cab signalling and automated driving systems which have been undergoing trials on both the Southern and London Midland Regions.   The basic signal repeating aws (sraws) provides a visual indication in the cab of the next signal ahead if it is within 250m of it and an indication of the signal which has just been passed until the train reaches to within 250m of the next signal.   It is an intermittent system in that the cab indications cannot change once the train has passed a signal until it approaches the next.   On the London Midland Region at Wilmslow the system has been developed into a full continuously monitored display with indications of speed limits.

Another system which can provide cab indications of permitted maximum speed and distance travelled but not signal indications uses track-mounted transponders.   A transponder consists of an electronic package built into a wood and glass fibre casing attached to the sleepers between the rails.   The electronic equipment is normally inactive and needs no external lineside power supply. It is brought to life by an inductive signal transmitted from a passing train by an underfloor aerial beneath the traction unit.   The transponder uses some of the energy transmitted to generate a 24Vdc supply to provide power to the solid state circuits which create coded signals which are transmitted back to the train.   The numerical codes can be used to provide a number of different messages, for example, location and speed limit details.   The messages received by the train are fed into a mini computer which will check the information received to see that it agrees with the known sequence for the route and the resulting information could be displayed on the driver's control panel in the form of distance travelled and the speed limit at a particular location.   The electronic equipment packed into a transponder is set during manufacture and cannot be altered afterwards so that each transponder can only transmit fixed information and thus cannot be used for transmitting variable messages about train signalling.

At one time it was thought that when BR entered the 100mph plus era some form of cab signalling would be essential but the 125mph trains are running without any special cab signalling facilities, with drivers relying on visual sightings of lineside colour-light signals supplemented by basic aws indications. The 150mph advanced passenger train (apt) however while still relying on basic aws and visual sighting of signals, will have a form of cab signalling in that a transponder installation will be employed on the apt route between Euston and Glasgow to provide the driver with speed limit indications at specific locations. It remains to be seen whether some form of continuous or intermittent cab signalling will be needed to supplement transponders. Despite the high speeds of trains the signals transmitted from the train to energise the transponder and the transponder's reply can be picked up in the fraction of a second available as a train passes the spot at 150mph. In some ways it can be likened to a beam of light (representing the signal transmitted from the train) being reflected by a series of mirrors (the transponder) to form a pattern of lights back to the train where the pattern can be read as a message.

Visual Display Units

On page 116 is illustrated a visual display unit (vdu) installed by London Transport in Rickmansworth signal cabin to show the track layout at Watford, together with signal indications, track circuit occupation, train operating details etc. BR has also adopted vdu equipment at London Bridge and other power signalboxes, although here they supplement normal track diagrams and are provided to allow signalmen and supervisors to display parts of the track diagram not under their control which it would be difficult for them to see because of the length of the main panel. The information is fed to the vdu from the train describer computer. Where trains are out of course it is useful for example for the signalman controlling the terminal platforms at say Charing Cross or Cannon Street to have a picture of train movement further down the line so that he can plan his moves accordingly. It would also be possible to display on the vdu sections of the track diagram from an adjacent signalbox assuming the right computer link, which would save telephone enquiries as to the whereabouts of late running trains. Vdus are also used from closed circuit tv to display information, for example as train arrival indicators in a passenger concourse.

Moorgate Control

In February 1975 a London Transport underground train on what was then the Northern City branch of the Northern Line from Drayton Park to Moorgate approached the dead-end underground platform at Moorgate but, instead of drawing to a stop, for some unaccountable reason the train continued at speed, seemingly under power, and collided heavily with the dead-end tunnel wall beyond the platform at Moorgate, causing considerable damage to the train and heavy loss of life. Following this accident the Ministry of Transport railway inspecting officers introduced new recommendations for speed checking devices at all underground dead-end stations to ensure that a similar accident

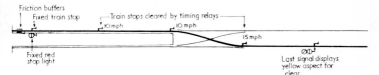

FIG 55 'Moorgate control' with train stop trip arms released by timing relays to ensure that train speed is reduced to prescribed levels at the approach to dead-end tunnel and certain other terminal stations on urban and underground railways.

could never happen again, either by a moment's inattention by a driver or in any other way. The new system applies to all London Transport underground terminal stations and to similar British Railways lines, as for example the Waterloo & City line of the Southern Region and to the Moorgate line itself, which is now part of the Eastern Region suburban routes from Welwyn Garden City and Hertford. Like London Transport stock the new Eastern Region electric trains are fitted with trip-cock train stop apparatus so that should they pass a signal at danger on the underground section they are automatically brought to a stop.

The form of control for a train approaching a terminal station is automatic in its action and depends on timing devices triggered by track circuits or treadles to ensure that trains have been brought down to the prescribed speed limits before the train stop and the related signals, if any, will clear. A series of train stops approaching the platform and along the platform are designed to clear only if train speed is reduced to about 10mph by halfway along the platform, while a fixed train stop just beyond the stop light at the stop mark together with a friction bufferstop should be capable of stopping a train if the driver failed to make a final brake application. Traction current limiting devices prevent a driver of an arriving train from applying power to accelerate. All the train stops approaching, and in the platform (and their associated time releases) are designed to stop a train before reaching the tunnel end wall should it exceed the prescribed speed on each section of approach. The timing relays are quite precise and if a speed of 10mph is ordained over a given section before a train stop will clear, the fall of the train stop to the clear position occurs only a yard or so ahead of the train; if train speed is much more than 1mph over the limit it is likely to be brought to a stop automatically by the trip apparatus.

London Transport also uses trip apparatus to prevent trains exceeding pre-determined speeds when approaching junctions with very short overlaps. This means that one train can approach closely to a junction while it is being occupied by a conflicting movement. Clearly with such a vital part played by the train stop apparatus it is essential for it to be in working order and trip tester lights can be seen at certain London Transport stations and also on the British Railways lines where trains are fitted with trip-cock apparatus, for example Euston–Watford, Waterloo & City, Mersey and Great Northern suburban lines, to ensure that the trip arms are in position and correctly adjusted. The test lights are initiated from track circuit occupation when the train approaches the test point and the trip arm, if in the correct position, engages a switch on the track which extinguishes the test light.

More Automation

It seems likely that the present four-aspect signalling system will survive in its basic form as long as there is a need for lineside signals, although the higher speeds over 100mph have already brought an expansion to six aspects to give more positive advanced warnings of lower speed divergences at junctions ahead as described at the beginning of this chapter.

Other developments in signalling equipment will be directed to the continued elimination of human error and advances in automation. Computers will play an increasingly important part in signalling control, although it will take many years of proving before they replace conventional relays or mechanical components in the vital interlocking equipment. London Transport for example is testing a computer to control signals and points automatically but only in conjunction with its well-tried mechanical interlocking machines which provide the final safeguard to prove the integrity of a route. Similarly, at least in the forseeable future, whatever forms of automation might be adopted by British Railways, route relay interlocking equipment will continue to be at the heart of BR signalling both on grounds of cost and reliability. Computers are relatively new to signalling applications and at present only serve for supervisory, recording and non-vital functions. They can be programmed with train service information so that in the event of disruption alternative solutions can be offered quickly to the supervisory staff, but it is not possible economically to justify every possible situation being programmed in a computer.

Nevertheless, in long term experiments British Railways research department is already looking at electronic solid state switching as a possible replacement for the conventional electro-magnetic signalling relay. But, in order to prove the absolute integrity of such devices in vital interlocking circuits, research work in this field is likely to be prolonged and it could well be another decade before such equipment could be employed for route setting purposes.

In Britain and in other countries experiments are already in hand with automated route setting, and clearly developments in one country will be watched with interest in others where traffic conditions and requirements are similar. Already in Switzerland, for example, experiments are well advanced in automated route setting at principal junctions in which the initial figure of the train number is identified by the train describer and can be used to programme the route setting equipment to set up the correct route for the train. Another form of manual route setting on trial in Switzerland in conjunction with a computer is a keyboard rather like a typewriter keyboard in which the signalman taps out on the keys coded instructions to the equipment to set a route from one part of the layout to another. This means the need for the large operator's control panel with the route setting buttons spaced in their geographical locations is obviated and the signalman's controls are in fact reduced to the size of a typewriter itself. With miniaturisation of track diagram indication panels signalling control rooms could thus become much smaller yet still control many miles of route.

At the end of the last chapter we saw how simple radio communication is on trial on the Ravenglass & Eskdale Railway for signalling purposes. In more sophisticated form, radio communication between signalboxes or power signalling centres and trains on the move is on trial on several railways, and BR is to conduct experiments with GN suburban electric trains running from Kings Cross and Moorgate to see how new radio technology stands up to rail use. The experiments consist not only of spoken messages but also data transmission which will appear as a message shown on a visual display unit in the driver's cab in the case of messages from a signalling control centre, or on the signalman's panel for messages from trains. Messages will be automated in that only the train for which a data message is intended will have it displayed in the cab. Moreover the identity of the train will be transmitted as part of messages from trains to signalling centre. As a basic system, radio communication could replace lineside signalpost telephones, but in more complex form there is a possibility of its use for train signalling on lightly-used lines where centralised power control and lineside signals could not be justified economically. Systems could be automated to supervise driving control, and in conjunction with transponders (see page 129) could be used to report a train's position without long lengths of track circuiting. Only in the last decade or so has radio communication become sufficiently versatile and reliable (developed as

Hot axlebox read-out unit in modern BR power signalling centre. The counter displays indicate the position of axles with hot bearings by number from the front of the train concerned, and the lights below show on which side of the train. Up to four hot axleboxes can be recorded on each train.   [British Railways.

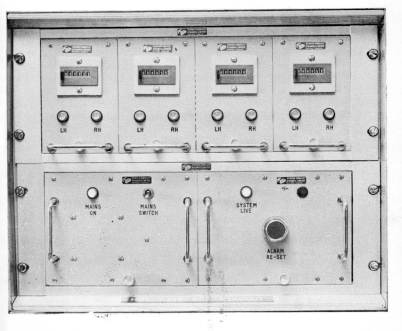

part of space technology) to be considered for rail use. Now it must be proved.

There will also be developments in automated train surveillance systems since with the development of centralised signalling control rooms there is now nobody at local stations or on open sections of line to watch each train as it passes, to make sure that all is in order and that there are no hot axleboxes, shifting loads or flapping sheets. Already hot axlebox detectors are in wide use in many parts of the world and experiments are in hand to devise other detectors which can pick up vehicles with dragging brakes, vehicles with a potentially dangerous wheel flat, and loads which have shifted on a freight wagon, identifying them in two ways, one an infra-red position detector to show if they have broken loose and slipped to a position where they might be on the edge of a wagon possibly in a position to be struck by another train, and another which records the weight balance of a wagon which might have altered to a dangerous degree in which the wagon might be derailed. The latter involves what is known as a wheel weight comparator which records the weight on each wheel of the wagon to ensure that it is even. This last device has been successfully tried at very low speeds but one of the problems in assessing weights at high speed are the general movement shocks of a train travelling at speed.

The automated railway is already here, in London, in America and in Japan. It is technically possible to have trains without drivers, controlled by signalling equipment, in contrast to the first trains which had drivers and very few signals. Experiments are in hand in many other parts of the world. But new developments take time to ensure their integrity. Railway signalling did not appear overnight; it has been evolved and proved over many years within fail-safe principles which make railways the safest form of travel in the world. It is a salutory thought that in 1976 and 1977 not a single passenger was killed in a train accident in Great Britain, a tribute indeed to signalling and other rail technology.

Appendix 1—British Railways Standard Signalbox Bell Codes

Class of Train	Description	Code
—	Call attention ... . Is line clear for:	1
1	Express passenger train, postal train, newspaper train, or breakdown van train or snow plough going to clear the line, or light locomotive going to assist disabled train Officers' special train not requiring to stop in section	4
	Electric express passenger train (not applicable on Southern Region)	4—2
2	Ordinary passenger train, mixed train, or breakdown van train or snow plough NOT going to clear the line	3—1
	Electric ordinary passenger train (not applicable on Southern Region)	3—1—2

Class Train	Description	Code
3	Express parcels train composed of vehicles permitted to run at 90mph or over	1—3—1
4	Freightliner train...	3—2—5
	Parcels train, Company or express freight train composed of vehicles permitted to run at 75mph or over	3—1—1
5	Empty coaching stock train (not specially authorised to carry Class 1 headcode)	2—2—1
	Electric empty coaching stock train (not applicable on Southern Region)	2—2—1—2
6	(a) Fully-fitted Company or block train, parcels train or milk train	5
	(b) Ordinary fully-fitted express freight train	4—1
7	Express freight train, not fully-fitted, but with brake force not less than that shown in Section E of the Working Manual for Rail Staff	1—2—2
8	Freight train, not fully-fitted, but with brake force not less than that shown in Section E of the Working Manual for Rail Staff	3—2
9	Unfitted freight train (where specially authorised) ...	1—4
	Freight train, officers' special train or engineer's train requiring to stop in section	2—2—3
10	Light locomotive, light locomotives coupled or locomotive with brake tender(s)	2—3
	Locomotive with not more than two brake vans	1—1—3
—	Trolley requiring to go into or pass through tunnel	2—1—2

Description	Code
ain entering section	2
ain which can pass an out-of-gauge or exceptional load similarly signalled on the opposite or an adjoining line	2—6—1
ain which cannot be allowed to pass an out-of-gauge load of any description on the opposite or an adjoining line between specified points	2—6—2
ain which requires the opposite or an adjoining line to be blocked between specified points	2—6—3
pposite line, or an adjoining line used in the same or opposite direction, to be blocked for passage of train conveying out-of-gauge load ...	1—2—6
it of gauge load requiring to pass in wrong direction	1—6—2
ain approaching (where authorised)	1—2—1
ncelling	3—5
st train signalled incorrectly described	5—3
arning Acceptance	3—5—5
he now clear in accordance with Regulation 4 for train to approach ...	3—3—5
ne occupied acceptance (permissive block)...	2—4—3
ne clear to home signal (permissive block)	4—3
ain out of section, or Obstruction Removed	2—1
ocking back inside home signal	2—4
ocking back outside home signal	3—3
ain or vehicles at a stand	3—3—4
comotive arrived	2—1—3
ain drawn back clear of section	3—2—3
struction danger	6
ain an unusually long time in section	6—2
op and examine train	7
ain passed without tail lamp	9 to box in advance; 4—5 to box in rear.
ain divided	5—5

Description	*Code*
Shunt train for following train to pass	1—5—5
Train or vehicles running away in wrong direction	2—5—5
Train or vehicles running away in right direction	4—5—5
Opening of signalbox	5—5—5
Closing of signalbox	7—5—5
Closing of signalbox where section signal is locked by the block ...	5—5—7
Testing block indicators and bells	16
Shunting into forward section	3—3—2
Shunt withdrawn	8
Working in wrong direction (where authorised)	2—3—3
Train clear of section (double line)	5—2
Train withdrawn (double line)	2—5
Release token (electric token single line)	5—2
Token replaced (electric token single line)	2—5
Transference of tokens (single line)	4—4—4—4
Distant signal defective	8—2
Home signal defective	2—8

Appendix 2—Signalbox Lever Colours

(*Some colour schemes are obsolete; others are not used on all Regions*)

Lever colour	Function
Red	— Stop signals, shunting signals
Yellow	— Distant signals
Black	— Points
Blue	— Facing point locks; clearance bars; bolt block
Brown	— Level crossing bolt lock, gate stops and wickets
Green	— Gongs; electrical ground frame release; direction lever; mechanical indicators for barrow crossings; King levers
Black and White Chevrons (Pointing up for up lines down for down lines)	— Detonator placers
Blue / **Black**	— Facing point lock and points worked from one lever
Blue / **Brown**	— Electrical ground frame release; direction levers
Brown (white stripes)	— King levers
Red (three narrow white stripes)	— King levers
Red / **Yellow**	— Stop and distant signals worked from one lever (eg intermediate block signals)
Red / **Black**	— Relief line stop signals (WR only)
Yellow / **Black**	— Relief line distant signals (WR only)
Red (with white stripe)	— Stop signal electrically released from another box (eg Line Clear Release)
Yellow (with white stripe)	— Distant signal electrically released from another box (eg indicator working with electric release on lever)
Red / **Brown**	— Direction lever
White	— Spare

Published by Ian Allan Ltd., Shepperton, Surrey and printed in the United Kingdom by
The Press at Coombelands Ltd., Addlestone, Surrey KT15 1JN.

WAKEFIELD   METROPOLITAN   DISTRICT   LIBRARIES

This book must be returned by the last date entered above.

An extension of loan may be arranged on request if the book
is not in demand.

Readers should make the fullest use of the library service,
asking for any books and information they need.

071 100 898 121 01 1F   71231/4